Fourth Workshop on Metaphor in NLP 2016

Held at the 2016 Conference of the North American Chapter of the Association for Computational Linguistics: Human Language Technologies (NAACL HLT 2016)

San Diego, California, USA
17 June 2016

ISBN: 978-1-5108-2519-2

Printed from e-media with permission by:

Curran Associates, Inc.
57 Morehouse Lane
Red Hook, NY 12571

Some format issues inherent in the e-media version may also appear in this print version.

Printed by Curran Associates, Inc. (2016)

For permission requests, please contact the Association for Computational Linguistics
at the address below.

Association for Computational Linguistics
209 N. Eighth Street
Stroudsburg, Pennsylvania 18360

Phone: 1-570-476-8006
Fax: 1-570-476-0860

acl@aclweb.org

Additional copies of this publication are available from:

Curran Associates, Inc.
57 Morehouse Lane
Red Hook, NY 12571 USA
Phone: 845-758-0400
Fax: 845-758-2634
Email: curran@proceedings.com
Web: www.proceedings.com

NAACL HLT 2016

The Fourth Workshop on Metaphor in NLP

Proceedings of the Workshop

17 June 2016
San Diego, CA, USA

Introduction

Metaphor processing is a rapidly growing area in NLP. Characteristic to all areas of human activity (from poetic to ordinary to scientific) and, thus, to all types of discourse, metaphor becomes an important problem for NLP systems. Its ubiquity in language has been established in a number of corpus studies and the role it plays in human reasoning has been confirmed in psychological experiments. This makes metaphor an important research area for computational and cognitive linguistics, and its automatic identification and interpretation indispensable for any semantics-oriented NLP application.

A growing number of NLP researchers are now working on metaphor. The goal of our workshop series on Metaphor in NLP is to provide a venue for an annual focused meeting to discuss issues on its computational modeling and methodologies for evaluation, as well as to place the phenomenon within the wider scope of the work done by the NLP community and relate it to the most recent research trends. The First, Second, and Third Workshops on Metaphor in NLP were co-located with NAACL-HLT 2013, ACL 2014, and NAACL-HLT 2015, respectively, and their programs featured many interesting and high quality presentations that were focused on metaphor identification, interpretation, affect in metaphor and real-world applications of metaphor processing. The workshops also featured cross-disciplinary invited talks that addressed metaphor and action (Prof. Jerome Feldman); an artificial intelligence approach to metaphor (Prof. John Barnden); metaphor in eighteenth-century British literature (Prof. Brad Pasanek); metaphor in clinical psychology (Dr. Rebecca Resnik); and lexical resources that could support metaphor processing (Prof. Martha Palmer, Prof. James Martin, and Dr. Susan Brown).

This year's workshop is the fourth Metaphor in NLP workshop; it features both continued development of the themes we observed in previous years, and new foci reflecting the trends in the larger NLP field. Thus, exploration of conceptual and affective features for metaphor identification continues in the 2016 papers, with the new focus on word-embedding based semantic representations (Rai, Chakraverty, and Tayal; Dinh and Gurevych; Haagsma and Bhjerva). Exploration of additional machine learning methods is the focus of a number of contributions to this year's workshop: conditional random fields are utilized by Rai et al, while Dinh and Gurevych present experiments using neural networks. J. Lederer presents a corpus-based study on mining metaphors from specific source domains (such as Ship, Weather, and Health) in target-domain discourse on Economy, using a sequence of collocation analyses. T. Veale presents a study in metaphor generation, gathering human ratings of interestingness, insightfullness and symbolism for metaphors generated automatically using a structured knowledge base about real and fictional personalities from popular culture.

This year's workshop additionally features guest presentations of papers on the topic of metaphor that were accepted to appear at NAACL and ACL main events in 2016. Both the talks address metaphoricity of verbs: Koper and Shulte im Walde discuss identification of non-literal usages of German particle verbs, while Beigman Klebanov, Leong, Shutova, Gutierrez, and Flor discuss identification of metaphorically used verbs using semantic classifications.

Two distinguished researchers working on human processing of metaphor at the Cognitive Science department of University of California in San Diego will give the invited talks at the workshop. Lera Boroditsky will talk about "Metaphors we think and feel with", and Seana Coulson will present her work on metaphor, conceptual blending, and creativity in the talk "Creative language: Metaphor and conceptual blending".

We wish to thank everyone who showed interest and submitted a paper, all of the authors for their contributions, the members of the Program Committee for their thoughtful reviews, the invited speakers for sharing their perspectives on the topic, and all the attendees of the workshop. All of these factors contribute to a truly enriching event!

Workshop co-chairs:
Beata Beigman Klebanov, Educational Testing Service, USA
Ekaterina Shutova, University of Cambridge, UK
Patricia Lichtenstein, University of California, Merced, USA

Organizers:

Beata Beigman Klebanov, Educational Testing Service, USA
Ekaterina Shutova, University of Cambridge, UK
Patricia Lichtenstein, University of California, Merced, USA

Program Committee:

Shlomo Argamon, Illinois Institute of Technology, USA
John Barnden, University of Birmingham, UK
Danushka Bollegala, University of Liverpool, UK
Susan Brown, Univeristy of Colorado, USA
Paul Cook, University of New Brunswisk, Canada
Gerard de Melo, Tsinghua University, China
Ellen Dodge, ICSI, UC Berkeley, USA
Jonathan Dunn, Illinois Institute of Technology, USA
Anna Feldman, Montclair State University, USA
Jerry Feldman, University of California at Berkeley, USA
Michael Flor, Educational Testing Service, USA
Andrew Gargett, University of Birmingham, UK
Mark Granroth-Wilding, University of Cambridge, UK
Yanfen Hao, TrustScience, Edmonton, Alberta, Canada
Eduard Hovy, Carnegie Mellon University, USA
Anna Jamrozik, University of Pennsylvania, USA
Hyeju Jang, Carnegie Mellon University, USA
Valia Kordoni, Humboldt University Berlin, Germany
James H. Martin,University of Colorado at Boulder, USA
Saif Mohammad, National Research Council Canada, Canada
Behrang Mohit, Carnegie Mellon University, Qatar
Michael Mohler, Language Computer Corporation, USA
Preslav Nakov, Qatar Computing Research Institute, Qatar
Malvina Nissim, University of Groningen, The Netherlands
Diarmuid O'Seaghdha, University of Cambridge, UK
Thierry Poibeau, Ecole Normale Superieure and CNRS, France
Paul Rayson, Lancaster University, UK
Brian Rink, Language Computer Corporation, USA
Eyal Sagi, University of St. Francis, USA
Sabine Schulte im Walde, University of Stuttgart, Germany
Samira Shaikh, SUNY Albany, USA
Caroline Sporleder, Goettingen University, Germany
Mark Steedman, University of Edinburgh, UK
Gerard Steen, University of Amsterdam, The Netherlands
Tomek Strzalkowski, SUNY Albany, USA

Marc Tomlinson, Language Computer Corporation, USA
Yulia Tsvetkov, Carnegie Mellon University, USA
Tony Veale, University College Dublin, Ireland
Aline Villavicencio, Federal University of Rio Grande do Sul, Brazil
Andreas Vlachos, University of Sheffield, UK

Invited Speakers:

Lera Boroditsky, University of California, San Diego, USA
Seana Coulson, University of California, San Diego, USA

Table of Contents

Workshop Program

Friday, June 17, 2016

9:00–9:05

Opening remarks

9:05–10:00

Invited talk: Lera Boroditsky "Metaphors we think and feel with"

10:00–10:30

Finding metaphorical triggers through source (not target) domain lexicalization patterns
Jenny Lederer

10:30–11:00

Coffee break

11:00–11:30

NAACL paper: Beata Beigman Klebanov, Chee Wee Leong, Elkin Dario Gutierrez, Ekaterina Shutova and Michael Flor "Semantic classifications for detection of verb metaphors"

Friday, June 17, 2016 (continued)

11:30–12:00

Detecting novel metaphor using selectional preference information
Hessel Haagsma and Johannes Bjerva

12:00–12:30

NAACL paper: Maximilian Köper and Sabine Schulte im Walde "Distinguishing Literal and Non-Literal Usage of German Particle Verbs"

12:30–14:00

Lunch

14:00–14:30

Supervised Metaphor Detection using Conditional Random Fields
Sunny Rai, Shampa Chakraverty and Devendra K. Tayal

14:30–15:00

Token-Level Metaphor Detection using Neural Networks
Erik-Lân Do Dinh and Iryna Gurevych

Friday, June 17, 2016 (continued)

15:00–15:30

Round Up The Usual Suspects: Knowledge-Based Metaphor Generation
Tony Veale

15:30–16:00

Coffee break

16:00–17:00

Invited talk: Seana Coulson "Creative language: metaphor and conceptual blending"

Finding Metaphorical Triggers Through Source (Not Target) Domain Lexicalization Patterns

Jenny Lederer
San Francisco State University
1600 Holloway Ave. San Francisco CA 94132
lederer@sfsu.edu

Abstract

Some metaphorical mappings between source and target are obvious and appear in collocation patterns in natural language data. However, other metaphors that structure abstract processes or complex topics are trickier to investigate because the target domain is lexically divorced from the source. Using metaphors for the economy as a case study, this paper introduces new techniques to find metaphorical tokens when target and source relationships are nonobvious. Through novel methods, constellations of source-domain triggers are identified in the data and evaluated for metaphoricity and keyness and then grouped according to trigger potency.

1 Introduction

Collections of naturally occurring language data serve as repositories of metaphor and can be used to investigate lexical patterns indicative of conceptual metaphors. Since the introduction of sizable, computationally searchable corpora, metaphor researchers and corpus linguists have begun to probe questions of quantitative validity (Deignan 2005). This movement toward measurable indicators of metaphorical salience has allowed for increasing focus on the detection and numeration of conceptual metaphors, which is seen as a mechanism to shield conceptual metaphor research from ongoing methodological criticism (Gibbs 2015). For some, the validity of Conceptual Metaphor Theory (Lakoff and Johnson 1980) rests on movement away from a fine-grained qualitative analysis of exemplary data to more robust experimental and quantitative measures designed to gauge salience and nuanced details of how conceptual metaphors are lexicalized and expressed in natural discourse (Gibbs 2011; Deignan 2012).

Most analyses, however, are based on metaphorical data that are easy to mine. That is, examining a corpus for metaphorical data in which both source and target domain language is paired and collocated is a straightforward process. But, this method is not possible for some metaphorical concepts due to the nature of how target domains are instantiated. When a target domain like the ECONOMY is understood as a complex system and is based on multiple conceptual metaphors, direct lexical searches centered on target domain lexis will not recover all pertinent structural information about active source domains.

In addition to providing metaphor researchers supplementary strategies to validate impressionistic conclusions of model dominance, the methods modeled in this study offer several future lines of inquiry concerning the automated extraction of metaphorical data. The programmed extraction of metaphorical tokens is not only of interest to corpus linguists and metaphor researchers but is also a focus of attention in natural language processing and computational linguistics (Babarczy et al 2010; Tang et al. 2010). A subgroup of these researchers is focused on the automatic detection of metaphorical tokens in relation to the system of conceptual metaphors that structure a given language (cf. Shutova et. al. 2013; Dodge et al. 2015).

In this study, I offer a new mining technique centered on source, rather than target, language. The conceptual metaphors used to understand the economy are overwhelmingly activated by a particular group of metaphorical tokens. That is, specific frames that structure the economy are linked to a subset of lexemes, which consistently appear

Proceedings of The Fourth Workshop on Metaphor in NLP, pages 1–9,
San Diego, CA, 17 June 2016.

metaphorically and occur more frequently in economic discourse than in the general corpus. In this paper I will probe a subgroup of these metaphors including ECONOMY IS A SHIP and ECONOMY IS A WEATHER EVENT through an examination of source domain lexicalization patterns. I describe a systematic method of pulling common collocates of source domain labels from a general corpus, and then introduce new techniques to evaluate and group these metaphor triggers. In the case of the economy, a subset of source-domain triggers are habitually used metaphorically and occur more frequently in a corpus of economic discussion from *The Economist* magazine than in nonspecific English discourse. This relative frequency differential is assessed through a 'keyness score', which is a numerical measure of how frequent, on average, metaphorical triggers occur in the restricted corpus compared to the baseline corpus. Words that consistently activate the metaphorical source domain fit into a category of 'super triggers' and can then be used to mine additional corpora for more metaphorical data. Background

For quite some time, metaphor analysts have been engaged in automated data extraction of one kind or another. In most cases, methodological approaches focus on target domain language. For instance, Oster (2010) relies on collocation patterns in a nonspecific corpus to show which lexical units are most associated with metaphorical description of the emotion fear. Oster gathers co-occurrence information – the lexical units that most frequently collocate with *fear* – to find target-specific metaphorical expressions. She uses the results of collocation searching to build a source-domain ontology, arguing that the most "relevant" metaphors are those evoked by the highest number of linked linguistic expressions (p.742). For example FEAR IS SOMETHING INSIDE THE BODY is evoked more frequently than is FEAR IS AN ANTAGONIST. Some metaphors, however, such as FEAR IS FIRE are more creatively produced because they are linked to a larger set of linguistic expressions. In Oster's approach, frequency information combines with lexical co-occurrence data to produce a source domain's "productivity and creativity index" (p. 748) – additional parameters by which source domains can be compared.

Following a similar semi-automated approach, investigators working on the MetaNet project have engaged in a corpus-driven, lexical approach to researching the alignment between target domain expressions, source domain frames, and the grammatical constructions that blend the two (David, et al. 2014; Stickles et al. 2014). Target and source word pairs, such as *alleviate poverty*, in which the source domain of DISEASE is evoked to understand the target domain POVERTY, are used to examine the frequency of one source domain in relation to another. Through these source-target pairings, the frequency of activation of individual frames can be compared to other frames within the same source domain. For instance, in the British National Corpus, Stickles et al. (2014) show how poverty is more frequently discussed as a disease than as a basic harm. And, when understood as a disease, speakers are more likely to discuss the treatment of the affliction of poverty than the diagnosis of the disease of poverty. Thus, at a macro level, the corpus results lead to the conclusion that AFFLICTION and TREATMENT roles in the source domain are more salient than is the role of DIAGNOSIS (Stickles et al. 2014).

The commonality among most corpus-based approaches to metaphor research, whether through manual searching, sorting, and collection or semi-automated searching based on collocation patterns, is the focus on the target domain. In all cases described above, researchers use lexical items indicative of the target domain to find instances of conceptual metaphors. Oster's collocations searches rested on the word *fear* in order to find semi-fixed expressions like *fight fear*. Likewise, the data mining approach taken by Stickles et al. was to look for common collocates of the word *poverty*, such as *spread*, *alleviate*, and *fight*.

Many target domains, however, cannot be thoroughly investigated by searching a corpus for collocates of target lexemes because not all target language occurs near or next to source domain triggers. This is the case for metaphorical concepts that are fundamentally understood as processes not as entities, and most target domains, like the economy, are built on extremely complex conceptual ecology. Thus, the ease with which metaphorical structure can be exposed has to do with the relationship between source-domain language and the structural character of the target domain. When the target domain is cognitively complex and lexically divorced from the source, target-domain directed searching limits the extraction of relevant data.

Because of the constraints imposed by manual searching and the lexical division between source and target triggers, metaphor researchers in corpus linguistics have turned to alternative approaches (Koller et al., 2008; L'Hôte 2014; Demmen et. al. 2015). Demmen et al. (2015) use a semi-automated corpus-based approach to research "violence metaphors" active in discourse on cancer. In their method, repeated source domain verbs like *fight*, *battle*, and *struggle*, identified through manual searching, are grouped according to predetermined semantic fields such as "warfare" or "damaging and destroying" (p.211). These fields come from an adapted version of the UCREL2 Semantic Analysis System (USAS) tagger (Rayson et al. 2004) in *Wmatrix* (Rayson 2008). Their identification of relevant semantic fields, and the lexis associated with each, yields additional search tokens such as *destroy* and *shatter*, which serve as supplementary source domain triggers used to locate further metaphorical tokens in cancer discourse. This focus on the identification of source-domain language leads to a greater diversity of identified metaphorical lexis, feeding a systematic comparison of particular metaphorical tokens across groups of speakers and across genres of data. However, the use of pre-specified semantic domains can constrain the types of search tokens yielded because the resulting lexis is, for the most part, homogenous in nature –sets of synonymous verbs.

Like these studies, my methodology moves away from a target lexis focus, querying metaphorical language through a concentration on source language. However, the methods described below differ significantly from previous corpus-based approaches. Instead of relying on pre-specified semantic fields in the collection of candidate metaphor triggers, I use corpus collocation patterns to gather candidate triggers. This methodology results in a frame-based collection of candidate search terms, as opposed to a definition-based collection, resulting in a more comprehensive compilation strategy.

1.1 A Case Study: The Economy

As a target domain, the economy, along with basic understandings of business and finance, have been well researched within metaphor analysis both in and out of academia. Because the metaphors used to structure economic thinking are well understood, it serves as a good case study to investigate the ways in which the metaphors are instantiated in natural discourse. All data referenced in this paper comes from a 2,084,650 token corpus built from the business and finance sections of *The Economist* magazine (2008-2015).

The economy, as a complex, abstract system, does not have a particularly unique metaphorical structure. Systems of all kinds, such as social organizations, governments, corporations, climate, and physical organisms are understood primarily through the same sets of metaphors. These metaphors all have one thing in common: The source domains represent different instantiations and elaborations of material structures vis-à-vis the primary metaphor ABSTRACT SYSTEMS ARE PHYSICAL STRUCTURES. The structures that serve as subcases of this superordinate metaphor, however, vary: abstract complex systems can be understood through several types of concrete structure including machines, buildings, plants, and human bodies (Kövecses 2010: 156).

1.2 Metaphors for the Economy

The metaphors for the economy are varied and complex, as are the mapping within each metaphor. The partial metaphor list here comes from existing analyses (cf. McCloskey 1986; Boers 1997; Boers & Demecheleer 1997; Skorczynska & Deignan 2006; Kövecses 2010; Shenker-Osorio 2012). Illustrative data is from *The Economist* corpus.

ECONOMIC SYSTEMS ARE BUILDINGS

after the early 1990s financial ***crash****, in part because the government dealt swiftly with*
All three props have now ***collapsed****. In particular, as America's housing bust*

MONEY IS LIQUID

Footloose capital generates ***bubbles*** *as it* ***rushes in****, some complain, only to generate crises*

ECONOMY IS A WEATHER EVENT

Others blame ***deluges*** *of a more metaphorical kind:* ***floods of capital from abroad or floods of lending at home****.*
The euro crisis ***casts a chill over a sunnier economic picture*** *...*

ECONOMY IS A VEHICLE; ECONOMY IS A SHIP

Conditions are undeniably ***frothy***
today's traders are in truly ***uncharted (and very cold) waters****, and under*
The American economy is like a ***supertanker*** *that, even in* ***calm waters***

ECONOMY IS (AILING) HUMAN BODY

economy ***sneezes****, its trading partners* ***catch a cold****, are still in* ***surgery****, but today's* ***cure*** *may well be the source of tomorrow's* ***ills***

The overlapping nature of these related source domains helps explain the prevalence of lexical items that are compatible with more than one metaphor. Domain interdependence is hypothesized to, in part, explain how metaphorical lexis can activate more than one source domain, and the assignment of metaphorical tokens to one domain or another must be based on a close read of surrounding context.

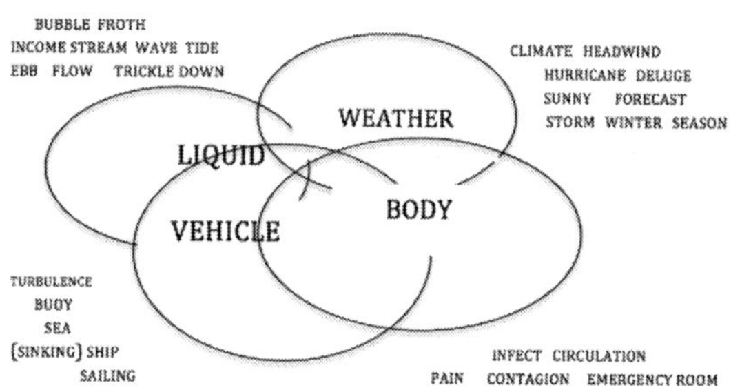

Figure 1: Multiple, overlapping source domains structure economic discourse and reasoning

2 Search Method

Unlike the investigation of a lexically-encoded metaphorical concept such as fear or poverty (Oster 2010; Stickles et al. 2014), a corpus approach directed at the economy cannot be comprehensive by searching for only target domain words such as *economic*, *finance*, and *business* because of the metaphorical complexity involved. Many source domain triggers in economic discourse are lexically removed from target domain language, and in this way, economic discourse mirrors the metaphorical disease language studied by Demmen et al. (2015) and Koller et al. (2008). Just as in these studies, I advocate for a new approach in which metaphors for the economy are investigated through the lexicalization patterns of the source domain. In this mixed-method approach, a small portion of the specialized corpus is qualitatively scanned for salient metaphors, and then quantitatively assessed by pulling source, not target, domain examples. However, unlike recently published corpus studies, I adopt an approach that integrates corpus collocation patterns. Rather than using a semantic ontology to build a set of source domain triggers, I pull triggers by looking at common collocates of source domain labels. Through the Sketch Engine interface (Kilgarriff et al. 2014), I compiled a 2,084,650 token corpus of *The Economist* data taken from articles in the Business and Finance sections of issues published between 2008 and 2015. In order to partially automate the identification of source domain language in this specialized corpus, I used collocation searching in a baseline corpus to identify source domain triggers (lexical items that activate one or more source domains used to structure the target concept). In this procedure, a source domain label serves as a collocation magnet to collect a list of frequent words associated with the specified domain. This method was employed to investigate source domains with tight constellations of lexical triggers.

To investigate the SHIP source domain, I searched the academic section of the Corpus of Contemporary American English (Davies 2008-) for the most frequent significant collocates of the word *ship* (9L, 9R; MI > 3). (An MI score is a statistical measure of lexical attraction in the corpus and an MI greater than 3.0 is interpreted as significant (Cheng 2012).) To find weather-related language, the same collocate search was carried out with the word *weather*. This technique produced a list of the 100 top collocates for each source domain label. These candidate source domain triggers were then evaluated for their metaphoricity (rate of metaphorical use) in relationship to economic discourse in the specialized corpus by manually scanning concordance lines.

3 Results

The search method described above yielded a set of 100 potential source domain triggers for the two economic metaphors: ECONOMY IS A SHIP and ECONOMY IS A WEATHER EVENT.

3.1 Seeding Source Domain Searches Using Common Collocates

I have established three distinct categories to classify source domain triggers in the specialized corpus. 'Trigger lexeme' is the term I use to indicate any lexical item in the specialized corpus that evokes one or more relevant source domains. Many words can function as trigger lexemes. Some are words very closely tied to a source domain frame; for example, the phrase *on life support* is directly tied to our understanding of hospitals, emergency rooms, and very sick patients, and can be used to activate the metaphor ECONOMY IS (AILING) HUMAN BODY. Other words, however, activate one source domain, but that source domain structures more than one target. This would be the case for a word like *circulation*, which can be used to describe the movement of money (MONEY IS LIQUID) but can also be used as a source domain trigger for a different metaphor like IMMIGRATION IS THE FLOW OF WATER. Thus *circulation* is only counted as a trigger when used in metaphorical description of the economy.

'Significant trigger lexemes' are lexical items that have a significant rate of use as a source domain trigger, quantified as a frequency of three or more metaphorical uses in reference to the target. These triggers must also be used in metaphorical reference to the target domain in at least 20% of the instances of total use, yielding a moderate to high rate of metaphoricity.

'Super trigger lexeme' refers to lexical items unique to the specialized corpus with a significant rate of metaphorical use in reference to the specified target domain (over 20%). Uniqueness is measured by a disproportionate use in the specialized corpus compared to a baseline corpus. To quantify uniqueness, I ranked individual lexical items through a basic algorithm, which I call a 'keyness score' (Ahmad 2005). In this measure, the frequency rate of the lexical item in the specialized corpus is divided by the frequency ratio of the item in a general corpus. Any item which occurs at a higher rate in the specialized corpus will measure at a keyness score greater than 1.0.

$$\text{keyness(term)} = \frac{F_{special}/N_{special}}{F_{general}/N_{general}}$$

Figure 2: 'Keyness' Formula (F=Frequency of item; N=Number of total tokens in corpus)

This measure quantifies the relative frequency of a particular lexical item in the specialized corpus (compared to a baseline) and allows lexical items to be both ranked by their relative frequency and numerically compared to one another.

3.1.1 The SHIP Source Domain

Trigger lexemes reside on a scale of potency in their relationship to the source domain. Some triggers loosely connect to the source domain, while others consistently evoke it. Figure 3 is comprised of a subset of the 100 top collocates of the lexical item *ship* in the academic section of COCA (9L, 9R; MI > 3). These are all words that evoke the SHIP frame. But, again, there is wide variation in whether or not these collocates are used as source domain triggers for the metaphor ECONOMY IS A SHIP.

Not Triggers	Insignificant Triggers	**Significant Triggers**	**Super Triggers**
CARGO*	SHIP	WATERS	CHANNEL*
PASSENGER*	PORT*	SEA	SINK*
NAVY	(vehicle) WRECK*	BOAT(s)	SHORE (up)
COAST*	CRUISE*	OCEAN*	STORM*
MERCHANT*	BOARD*	SAILED	ANCHOR*
VESSEL*	CREW*	BALLAST	SAIL*
DECK*	VOYAGE*		AGROUND
PIRATE*	HULL*		KEEL
TRANSPORT*	CAPTAIN*		
BAY*			
SAILOR			
HARBOR*			
FLEET*			

Figure 3. Categorized triggers for ECONOMY IS A SHIP

3.1.2 The WEATHER Source Domain

Figure 4 is comprised of a subset of the 100 top collocates (9L, 9R; MI > 3) of the lexical item *weather* in the academic section of COCA. These are all words that evoke the WEATHER frame. But, again, there is wide variation in whether or not these collocates are used as source domain triggers for the metaphor ECONOMY IS A WEATHER EVENT.

Not Triggers	Insignificant Triggers	Significant Triggers	Super Triggers
INCLEMENT			VAGARIES
SNOW*	STORMY	TERRAIN	CLOUDY
TORNADOES	WIND*	SEVERE	FORECAST*
	CLIMATE	ATMOSPHERE	FREEZE*
	WEATHER	CONDITIONS	WAVE(s)
	TEMPERATURE	SEASON*	STORM(s)
	RAIN*	OCEAN*	CHANNEL*
	WET	COLD	DRY
	WINTER*		FLOOD*
	HURRICANE(s)		SUNNY
	ICE		MILD
			COOL
			CALM
			HOT
			DROUGHT*
			CLOUD*

Figure 4. Categorized triggers for ECONOMY IS A WEATHER EVENT

Certain frequent lexical items in the discourse about weather such as the word *snow* are never used in metaphors for the economy; whereas, other words like *vagaries*, part of weather discourse but less frequent in general discourse, are consistently used with a metaphorical meaning in discussions of the economy.

3.1.2 Limitations

Even though source domain collocations yield a large quantity of metaphorical language, there are limits. Not all trigger lexemes can be found through this automated technique. Manually tagging a subset of *The Economist* corpus reveals that there are robust source domain triggers that are not frequent collocates of their source frame labels. That is, there are trigger lexemes that come from our understanding of ships and weather, which do not frequently co-occur with the word *ship* and *weather*, and the fact that these triggers exist shows the limitations in using a methodology that exclusively relies on source frame collocation magnets.

An additional obstacle to this automated approach is the great variability in how dense and connected the constellation of source domain triggers is within a given source domain. In contrast to the source domains of WEATHER and SHIP, the source domain of an UNHEALTHY HUMAN BODY is a lexically diffuse conceptual domain. That is, there is no fruitful source domain label to use as a collocate magnet in COCA. Thus, the automated technique of using collocation patterns to find source domain seed language does not work here. In this case, source domain triggers have to be directly collected from *The Economist* corpus in order to investigate the metaphor by searching for likely source domain triggers given the identified source frame.

Standout source domain triggers among this set are the words *healthy*, *recovery*, *contagion*, and *ailing*. These lexemes, which occur frequently in the data, have high percentages of metaphorical use in reference to economic concepts and significant keyness scores, meaning they are more frequently represented in economic discourse than in academic English.

Insignificant Triggers	Significant Triggers	Super Triggers
CODE BLUE	AUTOPSY	AILING
CHEST PAINS	CURE*	LIFE SUPPORT
EPIDEMIOLOGY	PAIN(s)	CONTAGION
TRANSFUSION	MEDICINE(s)	AILMENT
EMERGENCY ROOM	DISEASE(s)	RECOVERY
ILL	PULSE	HEALTHY
	SICK	
	HEALTH	

Figure 5. Categorized triggers for ECONOMY IS AN (AILING) HUMAN BODY

We can, to some extent, explain super triggers through the overlapping of source domains, as was illustrated in Figure 1. Figure 6 contains all the super triggers from the various metaphors investigated above. About half of the total super triggers are words are compatible with more than one source domain.

Concepts like *float*, *buoy*, *choppy*, *turbulent*, and *wave* are central to our understanding of the movement of water, the performance of a ship on the water, and the effect of inclement weather on the water. When we think about navigating a ship through bad weather, these are concepts that come to mind.

HEALTHY	CIRCULATION	EBB	CHANNEL
RECOVERY	FLOW	CLOUD	STORM
AILMENT	BUBBLE	DROUGHT	WAVE
CONTAGION	HEADWIND	HOT	FREEZE
LIFE SUPPORT	CHOPPY	CALM	FORECAST
AILING	TURBULENT	COOL	CLOUDY
TIDE	FIZZLE	MILD	VAGARIES
TURBULENCE	BUOY	SUNNY	
CIRCULATE	MUDDY	FLOOD	
FLOAT	FROTH/Y	DRY	

Figure 6. All collected super triggers for the three source domains: SHIP, WEATHER, HUMAN BODY

The motivated, yet semi-random, nature of this collection of super triggers should remind us that Conceptual Metaphor Theory is not predictive of how source domains will be lexicalized (Lakoff and Johnson 1980). Metaphorical mappings serve as a template to model the systematic nature of figurative language and metaphorical reasoning, and once conceptual metaphors are identified, the re-occurrence of specific source domains can be expected. But, there is no way to predict a priori exactly how a source domain will be evoked in natural discourse, nor is there a way to foresee what source domain language will be adopted into the speech community and used consistently as idiomatic jargon.

3.2 Lexical Divorce

Words evoking the target domain of metaphors for the economy are, of course, prevalent and frequent in economic discourse. There are 12 target triggers in the top 100 most frequent words in *The Economist* corpus. (Top 100 list includes both content and function words.) Not one source domain super trigger is in the top 100.

Bank* Invest* Market* Firm* Debt* Financ* Rate* Price* Capital* Growth* Economy* Money*

Figure 7. Twelve most frequent target lexemes

Lexical divorce between source and target is evaluated by the existence or absence of collocations of common source and target triggers. Source triggers are inevitably less frequent than target triggers because, while the target is invariable, the source domains are numerous. Thus, the source domain 'super triggers' identified in Figure 6 are not among the most frequent words used when discussing economic issues. The only source domain super trigger in the top 1000 most frequent words in *The Economist* corpus is *recovery* (rank: 425). A search of the top 5000 collocates of each target lexeme reveals few source domain super triggers co-occur near or next to these target words (9R, 9L; MI>3.00). Of all source super triggers found through the source domain collocation searches described above, only a small subset appear regularly or even semi-regularly near or next to a target domain word (within the 1000 most frequent collocates). Figure 8 displays this distribution. Of the 37 source domain super triggers, only 12 are even loosely collocated with the top twelve target domain triggers.

Target Trigger	Source Domain Trigger Collocates in top 1000 (9R, 9L; MI>3.00)
Bank*	HEALTHY, RECOVERY
Invest*	RECOVERY, FLOW, BUBBLE
Market*	RECOVERY, BUBBLE, FROTH/Y, CALM, COOL
Firm*	RECOVERY, FLOW
Debt*	RECOVERY, BUBBLE, WAVE
Financ*	RECOVERY, FLOW, BUBBLE
Rate*	RECOVERY, FLOAT, FORECAST
Price*	RECOVERY, BUBBLE
Capital*	HEALTHY, FLOW, FLOOD, DRY
Growth*	HEALTHY, RECOVERY, FLOW, FORECAST
Econ*	HEALTHY, RECOVERY, FLOW, BUBBLE, FORECAST
Money*	RECOVERY, FLOW, BUBBLE, HOT, FLOOD

Figure 8. Target lexemes paired with most frequent source domain triggers

These patterns confirm that target domain directed searching may not be a particularly efficient or effective way of finding source domain language, certainly not an effective technique to find source domain triggers with high rates of metaphoricity that do not occur near or next to target language. The distribution also indicates that lexical divorce between source and target triggers is a significant obstacle to those automated extraction systems which rely on close collocations between source and target lexis.

4 Conclusion

Metaphor is treated differently across research fields. Corpus linguists tend to be interested in lexical metaphors, defined as nonliteral lexis used in text. Cognitive linguists tend to be interested in conceptual metaphors –the hierarchical, abstracted system of metaphor. Researchers interested in natural language processing fall into both of these camps. But those of the latter school must contend with metaphorical source domain language that is lexically separated from target concept. This lexical divorce between source and target triggers is a substantial obstacle to automated metaphor identification systems because metaphor retrieval can't be based exclusively on pairings of source and target words.

In this paper, I have demonstrated a methodology to use nonrestricted corpus data to identify constellations of source domain lexis that serve as potential metaphorical triggers. This simple technique involves searching a baseline corpus for common collocates of identified source domain labels. Once collected, these lexemes associated with the source domain frame can then be evaluated for their metaphoricty –use in reference to the target concept- and their 'keyness' –relative frequency in topical discourse concerning the target domain. These two metrics allow for a systematic, comparative evaluation of source language along a scale of trigger 'potency'.

NLP efforts concerning metaphor can be furthered through the identification of 'significant' and 'super' source domain triggers–lexical items that reliably evoke a robust conceptual metaphor. The effort to build ontologies of conceptual metaphor, necessary for any adequate computational model of semantic processing, should occur alongside the identification of salient trigger language, and the construction of such systems will benefit from the methodologies outlined in this paper.

References

Ahmad, K. 2005. "Terminology in text", Tuscan Word Centre Workshop. Siena, Italy.

Babarczy, A., Bencze I., Fekete I., & Simon, E. 2010. The automatic identification of conceptual metaphors in Hungarian texts: A corpus-based analysis. *LREC 2010 Workshop. Proceedings.*

Boers, F. 1997. "No Pain, No Gain" in a free market rhetoric: A test for cognitive semantics? *Metaphor and Symbol*, 12 (4): 231-241.

Boers, F. , & Demecheleer, M. 1997. A few metaphorical models in (western) economic discourse. *Discourse and Perspective in Cognitive Linguistics*, 115-129.

Cheng, W. 2012. *Exploring Corpus Linguistics, Language in Action.* Routledge, England.

David, O., Dodge, E., Hong, J., Stickles, E., and Sweetser, E. 2014. *Building the MetaNet metaphor repository: The natural symbiosis of metaphor analysis and construction grammar.* The 8th International Conference on Construction Grammar (ICCG 8), Osnabrück, Germany.

Davies, M. 2008- The Corpus of Contemporary American English: 450 million words, 1990-present. Available online at http://corpus.byu.edu/coca/.

Deignan, A. 2005. *Metaphor and Corpus Linguistics.* Amsterdam: John Benjamins.

Deignan, A. 2012. Figurative language in discourse. *Cognitive Pragmatics.* Hans-Jörg Schmid, ed., 437-462.

Demmen, J., Seminoi, E., Demjén, Z., Koller, V., Hardie, A., Rayson, P. Payne, S. 2015. A computer-assisted study of the use of violence metaphors for cancer and end of life by patients, family carers and health professionals. *International Journal of Corpus Linguistics*, 20(2): 205-231.

Dodge, E., Hong, J., and Stickles, E. 2015. Deep semantic automatic metaphor analysis. The Third Workshop on Metaphor in NLP. Denver, CO.

Gibbs, R. W. 2009. Why do some people dislike conceptual metaphor theory? *Cognitive Semiotics* 5(1-2): 14–36.

Gibbs, R. W. 2011. Evaluating conceptual metaphor theory. *Discourse Processes,* 48(8): 529-562.

Gibbs, R. W. 2015. Counting metaphors: What does this reveal about language and thought? *Cognitive Semantics* (1): 55-177.

Gibbs, R. W. Forthcoming. *The Metaphor Wars.*

Kilgarriff, Adam, et al. 2014. The Sketch Engine: ten years on. *Lexicography*, 1–30.

Koller, V., Hardie, A., Rayson, P., Semino, E. 2008 Using a semantic annotation tool for the analysis of metaphor in discourse. *Metaphorik.de* (15): 141-160.

L'Hôte, E. 2014. *Identity, Narrative and Metaphor : A Corpus-Based Cognitive Analysis of New Labour Discourse.* London, Palgrave Macmillan.

McCloskey, D. N. 1986. *The rhetoric of economics.* Brighton, UK: Wheatsheaf Books and Harvester Press.

Omori, A. 2008. Emotion as a Huge Mass of Moving Water. *Metaphor & Symbol,* 23(2): 130-146.

Oster, U. 2010. Using corpus methodology for semantic and pragmatic analyses: What can corpora tell us about the linguistic expression of emotions? *Cognitive Linguistics,* 21(4): 727-763.

Rayson, P., Archer, D., Piao, S., & McEnery, T. 2004. The UCREL semantic analysis system. In *Proceedings of the workshop on Beyond Named Entity Recognition Semantic labeling for NLP tasks in association with the 4th International Conference on Language Resources and Evaluation (LREC 2004),* Lisbon, Portugal, 7–12.

Rayson, P. 2008. From key words to key semantic domains. *International Journal of Corpus Linguistics,* 13(4): 519–549.

Shenker-Osorio, A. 2012. *Don't Buy It: The Trouble with Talking Nonsense about the Economy.* Philadelphia, PA, PublicAffairs.

Shutova, E., Teufel, S., and Korhonen, A. 2013. Statistical matphor processing. *Computational Linguistics,* 39(2): 301-353.

Skorczynska, H. Deignan, A. 2006. Readership and purpose in the choice of economics metaphors. *Metaphor and Symbol*, 21(2): 87–104.

Stickles, E., Dodge, E., and Hong, J. 2014. *A construction-driven, MetaNet-based approach to metaphor extraction and corpus analysis*. The 12th meeting of Conceptual Structure, Discourse, and Language (CSDL 12), Santa Barbara, CA.

Tang, X., Qu, W., Chen, X., & Yu, S. 2010. *Automatic metaphor recognition based on semantic relation patterns.* International Conference on Asian Language Processing.

Detecting novel metaphor using selectional preference information

Hessel Haagsma and **Johannes Bjerva**
University of Groningen
The Netherlands

Abstract

Recent work on metaphor processing often employs selectional preference information. We present a comparison of different approaches to the modelling of selectional preferences, based on various ways of generalizing over corpus frequencies. We evaluate on the VU Amsterdam Metaphor corpus, a broad corpus of metaphor. We find that using only selectional preference information is enough to outperform an all-metaphor baseline classification, but that generalization through prediction or clustering is not beneficial. A possible explanation for this lies in the nature of the evaluation data, and lack of power of selectional preference information on its own for non-novel metaphor detection. To better investigate the role of metaphor type in metaphor detection, we suggest a resource with annotation of novel metaphor should be created.

1 Introduction

Within natural language processing (NLP), there has been an increasing interest in the processing of figurative language in recent years. This increasing interest is exemplified by the (NA)ACL workshops on metaphor in NLP, and shared tasks like SemEval-2015, Task 11, about sentiment analysis of figurative language in Twitter.

The main benefits of improved treatment of figurative language within NLP lie with high-level tasks dependent on semantics, such as semantic parsing. For example, in multilingual semantic parsing, one would like to see both the English 'This textbook costs an arm and a leg.' and the Dutch 'Dit lesboek kost een rib uit het lijf.' (lit. 'This textbook costs a rib from the body.') to be mapped to the same meaning representation, which should not include references to any of the body parts used in the idiomatic expressions.

In this paper, we focus on one area of figurative language processing, namely the detection of novel metaphor, and especially the utility of selectional preference features for this task. By doing this, we hope to answer a two-fold question: can selectional preference information be used to successfully detect novel metaphor? And how do generalization methods influence the effectiveness of selectional preference information?

2 Background

2.1 Types of metaphor in language

The first part of any work on metaphor processing is is to arrive at a definition for 'metaphor'.

A good starting point for this is the MIP framework (Pragglejaz Group, 2007), which has this as the most important criterion for metaphor: 'a lexical unit is metaphorical if it has a more basic contemporary meaning in other contexts than in the current context' (paraphrased). Where 'more basic' is defined as more concrete, related to bodily action, more precise, and historically older. This is a very broad definition, causing many meanings to be classified as metaphorical.

Examples of this are found in the VU Amsterdam Metaphor corpus, which is annotated using the MIPVU procedure (Steen et al., 2010), an extension of MIP. In the corpus, we find a wide range of

Proceedings of The Fourth Workshop on Metaphor in NLP, pages 10–17,
San Diego, CA, 17 June 2016.

metaphor from highly conventionalized metaphor, such as *have* in Example 1, to more clear metaphorical cases, like *rolling* in Example 2.

(1) Do the Greeks **have** a word for it?

(2) [...] the hillsides ceased their upward **rolling** and curved together [...]

Three general categories of meaning can be distinguished. The first type of contextual meaning is literal meaning, which is the most basic meaning of a word. This kind of meaning is generally the least problematic, since the meaning can be deduced from the lexicon. The second type of meaning is conventional metaphorical meaning, i.e. a non-basic meaning of a word, which is also in the lexicon or sense inventory.

Novel metaphors form a third type of contextual meaning, one which is non-basic, but is not accounted for by the lexicon either. These are the most problematic, since their meaning cannot be deduced by selecting the correct sense from a sense inventory.

Aligned with the distinction between conventional metaphor and novel metaphor is the distinction between word sense disambiguation and metaphor detection. That is, word sense disambiguation can be expected to cover literal and conventionalized metaphorical meanings, whereas metaphor processing is necessary to deal with novel metaphorical meanings.

We argue here that the most important application of metaphor processing approaches lies not with conventional metaphors, but with novel metaphors. This type of metaphor is the most problematic for other NLP applications, since it requires a deduction of meaning from outside the sense lexicon. Therefore, it requires a dedicated metaphor processing system, whereas more conventional metaphor can, in principle, be handled by existing WSD systems.

This is not to say that metaphor processing research should exclusively focus on novel metaphor, since insights about metaphor and metaphoricity can definitely be useful for improving the handling of conventional metaphor within a word sense disambiguation framework. Nevertheless, the approach proposed in this paper aims only to deal with novel metaphor. In addition, separating the treatment of novel and conventional metaphor avoids the possible pitfall of trying to solve two essentially different problems using the same method.

2.2 Selectional preference violation as a feature for metaphor detection

Because, by definition, we cannot use a pre-existing sense or meaning definition for novel metaphor, novel metaphor processing provides a new kind of challenge. On the other hand, with the ultimate goal of integrating figurative language processing in a semantic parsing framework, novel metaphor is the most problematic for deducing meaning, and is thus the most relevant and interesting.

Another important aspect of novel metaphors is that they tend to be less frequent than conventional metaphor (and literals). This has the advantage of making one feature commonly used for metaphor detection, selectional preference violation, more effective.

The idea of using selectional preference violation as an indicator of metaphoricity goes far back (Wilks, 1975; Wilks, 1978), and has been widely used in previous work on metaphor detection (Fass, 1991; Mason, 2004; Jia and Yu, 2008; Shutova et al., 2010; Neuman et al., 2013; Wilks et al., 2013).

Using selectional preference violation as a heuristic works well, but has the fundamental shortcoming that selectional preferences are based on frequency; selectional preference data are obtained from a corpus by counting how often words occur together in a certain relation. Metaphor, on the other hand, is defined by basicness of meaning, and not frequency of meaning. Although these two are correlated, there are also many cases where the figurative sense of a word has become more frequent than its original, literal sense.

The result of this is that metaphor detection systems based on selectional preferences erroneously classify low-frequent literals as metaphorical and high-frequent metaphors as literal. However, if we intend only to capture novel metaphors, the selectional preference violation approach is less vulnerable to these errors, since novel metaphors are less likely to be mistakenly classified as literal due to their lower frequency.

As such, we hypothesize that this feature, when used correctly, can be very useful for metaphor detection. To this purpose, we examine new ways of generalizing over selectional preferences obtained from a corpus.

3 Methods

Selectional preference information can be automatically gathered from a large, parsed corpus. This allows for counting the occurrences of specific pairs, such as 'evoke-excitement'. Based on this, we can then calculate conditional probabilities or a measure like selectional association (Resnik, 1993).

However, even a very large corpus will not yield full coverage of all possible pairs. This could cause the system to flag, for example 'evoke-exhilaration' as a selectional preference violation and thus as metaphoric, simply because this combination occurs very infrequently in the corpus.

The solution to this problem is to do some sort of generalization over these verb-noun pairs. One way of doing this is to perform clustering the verbs and nouns in semantically coherent classes. We test two clustering methods: Brown clustering (Brown et al., 1992), and a novel method, which relies on k-means clustering of word embeddings.

In addition to these clustering methods, we also look at using word embeddings directly in a classifier, in order to prevent the information loss inherent in a clustering approach. These approaches are compared to performance based on using the selectional preference information without any generalization and a most-frequent class baseline.

3.1 Corpus frequencies

Before we can apply generalization methods over selectional preferences, we need to gather selectional preference frequencies from a large corpus of English. We use a recent dump (13-01-2016)[1] of the English part of Wikipedia. The corpus was preprocessed in order to extract only the raw text using WikiExtractor[2], resulting in a raw text corpus of approximately 1.6 billion words.

We use Wikipedia because of its size, which should help reduce sparsity for word pair frequencies, its range of topics, which increases the coverage in terms of word types. The downside of using Wikipedia is that it contains only one genre, namely scientific or encyclopaedia-style text. In contrast, the data used for evaluation is taken from different parts of the BNC, which represent different genres. Nevertheless, we assume that the larger size and number of topics of the Wikipedia corpus compensate for this.

As a dependency parser, we use the spacy.io[3] Python library, because of its speed, high accuracy and ease-of-use. From the parsed corpus, all verb-noun pairs with the labels `nsubj` and `dobj` were extracted and counted. This yielded 101 million verb-subject triples of 14.0 million distinct types and 67 million verb-object triples of 7.8 million distinct types. The triples contained 175,630 verb lemma types and 1,982,512 noun lemma types.

3.2 Selectional preference metrics

Selectional preference information can be used in three ways: as a conditional probability, a selectional preference strength for the verb, and as selectional association between a verb and a noun. The conditional probability is defined as follows:

$$P(n|v) = \frac{P(n,v)}{P(v)} \approx \frac{c(n,v)}{c(v)} \tag{1}$$

Where $P(n|v)$ is the probability of seeing noun n occurring with verb v. This can be approximated by using the counts c from the corpus.

For the other two metrics, we follow Shutova (2010) in using the metrics proposed by Resnik (1993), selectional preference strength (SPS) and selectional association (SA). Selectional preference strength is the information gain of a verb. This is an indicator of how selective the verb is in the choice of its arguments, and could thus be useful in filtering out weak-preference verbs.

$$SPS(v) = \sum_{n \in N} P(n|v) * \log \frac{P(n|v)}{P(n)} \tag{2}$$

More directly useful is the selectional association (SA) measure, which is an indication of how typical a noun is in its occurrence with a certain verb. It is defined as follows:

$$SA(v,n) = \frac{1}{SPS(v)} * P(n|v) * \log \frac{P(n|v)}{P(n)} \tag{3}$$

[1]https://dumps.wikimedia.org/enwiki/20160113/

[2]http://medialab.di.unipi.it/wiki/Wikipedia_Extractor

[3]https://spacy.io

3.3 Clustering

For the Brown clustering, we use the pre-trained clusters from Derczynski et al. (2015). They provide clusterings[4] with different numbers of clusters, which makes it easy to find an optimal number of clusters. We use the clusters trained on 64M words of newswire text.

For k-means clustering of word embeddings, we use the GloVe word embeddings (Pennington et al., 2014), with 300 dimensions, trained on a 840B word corpus and cluster the embeddings of the top 400,000 most frequent words. Clustering is done using the k-means clustering implementation from scikit-learn (Pedregosa et al., 2011), with k-means++ initialization, a maximum of 500 iterations, and the best clustering out of 10 runs with random initialization in terms of inertia.

3.4 Word embeddings-based probability predictions

In the word embeddings-based learner setting, rather than doing generalization through clustering, we use the word embeddings for generalization directly. This is done by modelling the conditional probabilities directly, based on the word embeddings of the noun and verb involved. We expect this to benefit generalization, since it avoids the information loss inherent in clustering when dealing with distributed representations – clustering (and thus discretizing) such representations effectively removes any notion of similarity between representations.

We use a neural network implemented in Theano (Bergstra et al., 2010; Bastien et al., 2012) using Keras. As input, we take the concatenation of the distributed representations of each verb and its subject/object. The output of the network is a continuous variable, namely the log probability of the construction at hand. We use a single hidden layer containing 600 hidden units, with a sigmoid activation function. Optimisation is done using the ADAM optimiser (Kingma and Ba, 2014). The loss function used is the mean squared error. Dropout is applied as regularisation after the hidden layer ($p = 0.5$) (Srivastava et al., 2014). We use a batch size of 2,000 and train over the course of 200 epochs. The resulting predictions are used as the Predicted Log-Probability (P-LP) feature. Metaphor detection results using this feature are presented in Table 4.

3.5 Evaluation

We evaluate the approaches on the VU Amsterdam Metaphor corpus (VUAMC)[5]. The corpus is preprocessed by extracting all raw text, and marking each word with the attribute `function="mrw"`, which indicates a metaphor-related word, as metaphor.

This results in a corpus of 40,622 verbs, of which 23,069 have at least one subject or object relation. We split the data three-way: verbs with only a subject (13,466 pairs), verbs with only an object (3,913 pairs), and verbs with both a subject and an object (5,539 triples).

We use this corpus since it is the largest corpus with metaphor annotations available. The downside is that it includes a large number of very conventionalized metaphors, and there is no annotation of novel metaphor or a degree of metaphoricity.

Evaluation is performed using a logistic regression classifier, which takes one or more of the selectional preference-based features. The features used are: conditional probability, log probability, selectional preference strength and selectional association, for subject-verb and object-verb pairs, and based on corpus frequencies, predictions or clusterings. We use only those features which are available, i.e. for the subject dataset we only use the four features for subject-verb pairs, while in the subject-and-object dataset we use eight features, four based on the subject-verb pair and four based on the object-verb pair.

Model fitting and evaluation is done using 10-fold cross validation, and l2-regularization with strength 1 is applied. In case of missing data points (e.g. no cluster available for the verb/noun), the majority class (non-metaphor) is assigned. As a baseline, we calculate the score when classifying all items as metaphor.

In addition, we evaluate the effect of re-weighting examples. Beigman Klebanov et al. (2015), who also evaluated their metaphor detection system on the VUAMC, showed that re-weighting training examples can have a large impact on performance, due to the large class imbalance in the VUAMC (mostly

[4]http://derczynski.com/sheffield/brown-tuning

[5]http://www.vismet.org/metcor/documentation/home.html

Data	BL	CP	LP	P-LP	SPS	SA	All
Subject	**23.0**	0.0	0.0	0.0	0.0	0.0	1.3
Object	**50.8**	0.0	3.2	1.4	0.0	0.0	2.4
Both	**53.4**	0.0	18.1	0.7	0.0	2.3	32.1

Table 1: F1-scores on metaphor identification using selectional preference information without any generalization, with varying features. Features: all-metaphor BaseLine (BL), Conditional Probability (CP), Log-Probability (LP), word embeddings-based Predicted Log-Probability (P-LP), Selectional Preference Strength (SPS), Selectional Association (SA), combination of CP, LP, SPS and SA (All).

Data	BL	CP	LP	P-LP	SPS	SA	All
Subject	23.0	24.5	24.5	23.2	20.9	26.4	**33.6**
Object	50.8	**53.4**	45.6	49.2	49.0	51.2	47.6
Both	53.4	54.2	44.3	50.0	50.5	53.8	**57.8**

Table 2: F1-scores on metaphor identification using selectional preference information without any generalization, with varying features. Features: all-metaphor BaseLine (BL), Conditional Probability (CP), Log-Probability (LP), word embeddings-based Predicted Log-Probability (P-LP), Selectional Preference Strength (SPS), Selectional Association (SA), combination of CP, LP, SPS and SA (All). Re-weighting of training examples was applied.

non-metaphor). They find that re-weighting examples increases F1-score by sacrificing precision for a large increase in recall.

4 Results

In this section, we present the results of evaluating each of the approaches to modelling selectional preference information on the VUAMC, as described previously. Table 4 shows the results for metaphor detection without any form of generalization. Table 4 shows the same, but with re-weighting of examples.

The most striking difference here is the difference between the two sets of results. Without re-weighting, performance is poor. The classifier classifies almost everything as non-metaphorical for the subject and object datasets, and for the subject-object dataset, even the best feature set is still far below the baseline.

In contrast, we see that performance with re-weighting is a lot better for all datasets. For the subject and subject-object datasets, the setting with all features performs best, out-performing the baseline by 10.6% and 4.4% respectively. For the object dataset, however, performance is highest with only the most basic feature, the conditional probabilities, out-performing the baseline by 2.6%. Clearly, the re-weighting of of examples enables the classifier to find a model that actually detects metaphor, rather than defaulting to a majority-class baseline.

Tables 5 shows the results for Brown clustering, Table 5 does the same for k-means clustering, and the P-LP column in Table 4 shows the results for word-embeddings based prediction. Since performance using all features and re-weighting of examples worked best in the no-clustering setting, we only report the results using these settings.

Results show that all generalization approaches fail to improve over the non-generalization setting. The Brown clustering seems to work better than the k-means clustering, which in turn yields slightly higher results than the predicted probabilities. The differences between the datasets are not affected by generalization, performance, relative to the baseline, is highest for the subject-only data, whereas it is lowest on the object-only data.

For both the Brown and k-means clustering, cluster size seems to only have a minor effect on performance, and no consistent pattern emerges from the results. That is, there is no cluster size which performs consistently better across data sets and/or clustering methods.

5 Discussion

The most prominent conclusion we can draw from the results is that, in the current set-up, generalization across selectional preference information using clustering or prediction does not work. Although the generalization approaches sometimes improve over the baseline, they never out-perform the best results from the no-generalization setting.

The idea behind generalization is that we sacrifice some information (about specific words) for a gain in robustness of the feature values, especially for less frequent words and word combinations. Here, clearly, the benefits do not outweigh the disadvantages. Since we explored a large range of cluster

Data	BL	80	160	320	640	1280	2560	5120
Subj	23.0	26.3	**28.8**	27.9	25.9	26.3	26.6	25.3
Obj	**50.8**	48.7	47.7	45.3	46.9	44.7	44.6	46.2
Both	53.4	52.7	52.8	53.7	54.3	53.5	54.3	**54.5**

Table 3: F1-scores on metaphor identification using Brown clustering for generalization, for varying numbers of clusters, using all available features. Re-weighting of training examples was applied.

Data	BL	80	160	320	640	1280	2560	5120
Subj	23.0	24.2	23.5	**30.7**	28.6	24.4	23.6	22.9
Obj	**50.8**	40.4	44.8	45.8	44.2	48.9	48.8	49.8
Both	**53.4**	49.8	48.2	50.4	49.2	47.6	50.4	49.5

Table 4: F1-scores on metaphor identification using word embedding-based k-means clustering for generalization, for varying numbers of clusters, using all available features. Re-weighting of training examples was applied.

sizes, which did not have a clear effect on detection performance, the root cause for this is likely to be the semantic coherence of the clusters. That is, either the clusters are not semantically coherent, or they are not coherent in such a way that they form a useful domain for metaphor detection.

As for the different datasets, we see a large performance difference in Table 4, where the model almost always defaults to a majority class classification in the object- and subject-only cases. Re-weighting the training data, however, removes this effect completely. Even for the subject-only data, which has the most skewed distribution (only 13% metaphor) the re-weighting model works well.

Looking at instances classified as metaphor by the best-performing system (57.8% F-score, Table 4) reveals three main things about the system performance and the nature of the evaluation data.

First, all datasets, but especially the subject- and object-only datasets contain a large proportion of pronoun subjects and objects, for which selectional preference information is not useful, unless pronoun resolution is applied. Since the metaphor annotation procedure does include resolving of referring expressions, this significantly hurts performance. An obvious improvement therefore would be to combine metaphor detection with coreference resolution.

Second, we find that a large part of the triples classified as metaphor contain a light verb, such as *have*, *make*, *take*, and *put*. Looking at the dataset as a whole reveals that 85-90% of the triples containing these verbs are classified as metaphor by the system. In the VUAMC, these verbs are often annotated as metaphor, since, due to their wide usage, they often occur in a sense that is not the most basic. It could be argued that these verbs, on the contrary, have such an eroded meaning that they are never metaphorical (Shutova and Teufel, 2010; Beigman Klebanov et al., 2014).

Third, we notice that the amount of novel metaphors in the VUAMC is minimal. Looking at instances correctly classified by the best-performing system yielded only one example of novel metaphor (Example 3). Here, the verb *escape* is used in a novel way; no matching sense is found in WordNet.

(3) [...] Adam might have **escaped** the file memories for years,

We hypothesized that selectional preference information can be used successfully for detection of novel metaphor, but the VUAMC contains all kinds of metaphor, including a large number of highly conventionalized metaphors. As such, even if the hypothesis is true, we cannot see this in the current evaluation setting. Unfortunately, this presents us from answering the research question posed in the introduction; it is still unclear whether selectional preference information is useful for detection of novel metaphor.

Due to the different kinds of metaphor in the corpus, the logistic regression model attempts to learn a model for all kinds of metaphor. This is not possible, and as such almost all instances get classified as the majority class, non-metaphorical. If novel metaphor could be successfully detected with the features used here, the regression learner might not produce a model that achieves this, since there is a large majority of conventional metaphor in the data.

In order to empirically evaluate how well these features work for novel metaphor, a corpus of novel metaphor, or a general corpus of metaphor with metaphoricity annotations is required. Considering that this is not available, an interesting course for future work would be to create such a resource, and use that for the evaluation of systems for novel metaphor detection.

This could be done as a completely new resource, but also as an extension of existing resources' annotation. The VUAMC for example, could be extended by annotating whether metaphorically used words are used in a novel sense, i.e. an out-of-vocabulary sense. This would fit nicely with the MIPVU procedure, which is already strongly dependent on a fixed sense lexicon. An alternative would be to annotate metaphoricity or 'novelty of metaphor' as scalar, based on human judgements. This would also allow resources to distinguish more easily between types of metaphor.

Acknowledgements

We would like to thank the anonymous reviewers for their insightful and constructive comments, and Beata Beigman Klebanov for pointing out the utility of re-weighting the training data.

References

Frédéric Bastien, Pascal Lamblin, Razvan Pascanu, James Bergstra, Ian J. Goodfellow, Arnaud Bergeron, Nicolas Bouchard, and Yoshua Bengio. 2012. Theano: new features and speed improvements. In *Deep Learning and Unsupervised Feature Learning NIPS 2012 Workshop*.

Beata Beigman Klebanov, Chee Wee Leong, Michael Heilman, and Michael Flor. 2014. Different texts, same metaphors: Unigrams and beyond. In *Proceedings of the Second Workshop on Metaphor in NLP*, pages 11–17.

Beata Beigman Klebanov, Chee Wee Leong, and Michael Flor. 2015. Supervised word-level metaphor detection: Experiments with concreteness and reweighting of examples. In *Proceedings of the Third Workshop on Metaphor in NLP*, pages 11–20.

James Bergstra, Olivier Breuleux, Frédéric Bastien, Pascal Lamblin, Razvan Pascanu, Guillaume Desjardins, Joseph Turian, David Warde-Farley, and Yoshua Bengio. 2010. Theano: a CPU and GPU math expression compiler. In *Proceedings of the Python for Scientific Computing Conference (SciPy)*, June.

Peter F. Brown, Peter V. deSouza, Robert L. Mercer, Vincent J. Della Pietra, and Jenifer C. Lai. 1992. Class-based *n*-gram models of natural language. *Computational Linguistics*, 18(4):467–479.

Leon Derczynski, Sean Chester, and Kenneth S. Bøgh. 2015. Tune your Brown clustering, please. In *Proceedings of RANLP 2015*, pages 126–133.

Dan Fass. 1991. met*: A method for discriminating metonymy and metaphor by computer. *Computational Linguistics*, 17(1):49–90.

Yuxiang Jia and Shiwen Yu. 2008. Unsupervised Chinese verb metaphor recognition based on selectional preferences. In *22nd Pacific Asia Conference on Language, Information and Computation*, pages 207–214.

Diederik Kingma and Jimmy Ba. 2014. Adam: A method for stochastic optimization. *arXiv preprint arXiv:1412.6980*.

Zachary J. Mason. 2004. CorMet: A computational, corpus-based conventional metaphor extraction system. *Computational Linguistics*, 30(1):23–44.

Yair Neuman, Dan Assaf, Yohai Cohen, Mark Last, Shlomo Argamon, Newton Howard, and Ophir Frieder. 2013. Metaphor identification in large texts corpora. *PLOS ONE*, 8(4).

F. Pedregosa, G. Varoquaux, A. Gramfort, V. Michel, B. Thirion, O. Grisel, M. Blondel, P. Prettenhofer, R. Weiss, V. Dubourg, J. Vanderplas, A. Passos, D. Cournapeau, M. Brucher, M. Perrot, and E. Duchesnay. 2011. Scikit-learn: Machine learning in Python. *Journal of Machine Learning Research*, 12:2825–2830.

Jeffrey Pennington, Richard Socher, and Christopher D. Manning. 2014. GloVe: Global vectors for word representation. In *Proceedings of EMNLP 2014*, pages 1532–1543.

Pragglejaz Group. 2007. MIP: A method for identifying metaphorically used words in discourse. *Discourse, Metaphor and Symbol*, 22(1):1–39.

Philip Stuart Resnik. 1993. *Selection and Information: A class-based approach to lexical relationships*. Ph.D. thesis, University of Pennsylvania.

Ekaterina Shutova and Simone Teufel. 2010. Metaphor corpus annotated for source-target domain mappings. In *Proceedings of LREC 2010*, pages 3255–3261.

Ekaterina Shutova, Lin Sun, and Anna Korhonen. 2010. Metaphor identification using verb and noun clustering. In *Proceedings of COLING 2010*, pages 1002–1010.

Ekaterina Shutova. 2010. Automatic metaphor interpretation as a paraphrasing task. In *Proceedings of ACL 2010*, pages 1029–1037.

Nitish Srivastava, Geoffrey Hinton, Alex Krizhevsky, Ilya Sutskever, and Ruslan Salakhutdinov. 2014. Dropout: A simple way to prevent neural networks from overfitting. *The Journal of Machine Learning Research*, 15(1):1929–1958.

Gerard J. Steen, Aletta G. Dorst, J. Berenike Herrmann, Anna Kaal, Tina Krennmayr, and Trijntje Pasma. 2010. *A method for linguistic Metaphor Identification: from MIP to MIPVU*. John Benjamins, Amsterdam.

Yorick Wilks, Lucian Galescu, James Allen, and Adam Dalton. 2013. Automatic metaphor detection using large-scale lexical resources and conventional metaphor extraction. In *Proceedings of the First Workshop on Metaphor in NLP*, pages 36–44.

Yorick Wilks. 1975. A preferential, pattern-seeking, semantics for natural language inference. *Artificial Intelligence*, 6(1):53–74.

Yorick Wilks. 1978. Making preferences more active. *Artificial Intelligence*, 11(3):197–223.

Supervised Metaphor Detection using Conditional Random Fields

Sunny Rai*, Shampa Chakraverty*, and Devendra K. Tayal**
*Dept. of CoE, Netaji Subhas Institute of Technology, University of Delhi, India
**Dept. of CSE, Indira Gandhi Delhi Technical University for Women, India
{post2srai, apmahs.nsit}@gmail.com, dev_tayal2001@yahoo.com

Abstract

In this paper, we propose a novel approach for supervised classification of linguistic metaphors in an open domain text using Conditional Random Fields (CRF). We analyze CRF based classification model for metaphor detection using syntactic, conceptual, affective, and word embeddings based features which are extracted from MRC Psycholinguistic Database (MRCPD) and WordNet-Affect. We use word embeddings given by Huang *et al.* to capture information such as coherence and analogy between words. To tackle the bottleneck of limited coverage of psychological features in MRCPD, we employ synonymy relations from WordNet®. A comparison of our approach with previous approaches shows the efficacy of CRF classifier in detecting metaphors. The experiments conducted on VU Amsterdam metaphor corpus provides an accuracy of more than 92% and F-measure of approximately 78%. Results shows that inclusion of conceptual features improves the recall by 5% whereas affective features do not have any major impact on metaphor detection in open text.

1 Introduction

According to Merriam-Webster dictionary, *Metaphor*[1] is defined as "a figure of speech in which a word or a phrase literally denoting one kind of object or idea is used in place of another to suggest a likeness or analogy between them". As a literary tool, metaphor is popular and widely appreciated for the novelty and vividness it provides to an otherwise bland text. Contrary to the popular belief that metaphor is a tool for poetry, we see vast usage of metaphors in common parlance and even in scientific discourses like economics, security and politics. To achieve human computer interaction in the true sense, Natural Language Processing (NLP) systems need to be enhanced to process and understand metaphors and indeed, all kinds of figurative speeches in a continuous and open-domain text.

Interpreting metaphor in a language is a complicated task because the metaphorical meaning of a sentence depends on what a speaker actually wants to convey irrespective of the literal meaning of the words used (Searle, 1985). Thus, the literal meaning of words needs to be modified according to the contextual presentation of the metaphor (Gibbs, 1984). A linguistic metaphor indicates a domain that seems incongruous with the surrounding context but presents the underlying belief by re-conceptualization (Lynne and Deignan, 2003). Interestingly, we observe that unlike the process of metaphor interpretation, a linguistic metaphor can be detected by analyzing word properties and surrounding words i.e. context, to identify the incongruity it causes in the sentence without even examining the reconceptualization involved.

One of the earliest criteria for metaphor detection in a text was proposed by Wilks (1978). He stated that a metaphorical interpretation is made when literal interpretation makes no sense or is out of context, a condition known as violation of selectional preference, e.g.

My car drinks gasoline. (Wilks, 1978) *(a)*

However, metaphors occur even without violation of selectional preference, e.g.

All men are animals. (b)

[1]Merriam-Webster Dictionary, Metaphor: http://www.merriam-webster.com/dictionary/metaphor

Proceedings of The Fourth Workshop on Metaphor in NLP, pages 18–27,
San Diego, CA, 17 June 2016.

We also observe that combinations such as <*car, drink*> and <*drink, gasoline*> have very low co-occurrence frequency in a corpus. Lakoff and Johnson (1980) introduced another perspective and termed it as *conceptual metaphor* which regards metaphor as a product of cognitive phenomenon, and a way to explain abstract concepts such as *argument* by mapping them to concrete ones such as *war*, e.g.

The committee shot down her ideas one by one. (c)

Here in (c), the concrete concept, shot is used to explain the outright rejection of an abstract concept namely, ideas. Thus, conceptual features like abstractness (Turney *et al.*, 2011) or concreteness (Klebanov *et al.*, 2015), familiarity or rarity (Schulder and Hovy, 2014), imageability (Strzalkowski *et al.*, 2013) and sensory features (Gargett and Barnden, 2015) can improve automatic metaphor detection. Recently, Hovy *et al.* (2013) utilized word embeddings by Collobert *et al.* (2011) for capturing coherence and contextual features for supervised metaphor detection.

In this paper, we strive to provide a solution to the fundamental problem of metaphor processing *i.e. metaphor detection in text*. We propose a novel approach for binary classification of continuous, open-domain text into Metaphor or otherwise, using Conditional Random Fields (CRF) (Lafferty *et al.*, 2001) and a hybrid feature set. CRF has widespread applications in computational linguistics. In contrast with (Gedigan *et al.*, 2006) and (Turney *et al.*, 2011) which focus on verb and adjective centric metaphors, we extend the applicability of CRF to detect all kinds of metaphor. The idea is to develop an effective and computationally inexpensive process to filter out metaphors in an open text.

Unlike the majority of earlier works which focused on utilizing a particular type of feature set, we propose a rich and hybrid feature set to cover different aspects of a metaphor. We include features that pertain to sentence structure, psychological/conceptual properties of a word, affective interpretation which provides information on whether a word conveys a mood, a mental state or an emotion and the context of a word's usage using word embeddings. We analyze their effect on metaphor detection individually and in combination. We use Medical Research Council Psycholinguistic Database (MRCPD) (Wilson, 1988) for extracting conceptual features and WordNet-Affect (Strapparava and Valitutti, 2004) for extracting affective features. Further, we employ WordNet® (Fellbaum, 1998) to expand the limited coverage of psychological features in MRCPD. We utilize word embeddings (Huang *et al.*, 2012) as contextual features which provides semantic information for a word such as coherence, context, relatedness and analogy.

The paper is organized as follows. Section 2 provides an overview of existing literature on detection of metaphor. Section 3 delineates our proposed approach for metaphor detection, the feature sets used and extension of MRCPD by using WordNet®. We demonstrate our experiments and results in Section 4 and conclude our work in Section 5.

2 Related Work

Some of the earliest works in metaphor detection used concept of *violation of selectional preference* given by Wilks (1978). These include the system MIDAS (Martin, 1990) and met* (Fass, 1991), both of which are hand-coded rule-based systems. The work in (Mason, 2004) introduced a corpus based approach *viz.* CorMet to identify conventional non-literal phrases from a domain specific text. Recently, Baumer *et al.* (2010) proposed an approach based on selectional preference given by Resnik (1993) to detect conceptual metaphors.

Several researchers used *clustering based techniques* to identify non-literalness in text. Birke and Sarkar (2006) proposed the Trope Finder (TroFi) system to recognize verbs with non-literal meaning using Word Sense Disambiguation (WSD) and clustering. However, TroFi doesn't identify the type of non-literalness *i.e.* whether it is a metaphor or some other non-literal category such as idiom, sarcasm etc. Shutova *et al.* (2010) pointed out that a target concept associated with the same source concept are more likely to co-occur in similar lexico-syntactic environments. They proposed a clustering based technique using grammatical relations and lexical features to detect metaphors. In (Birke and Sarkar, 2007), the authors introduced the concept of Active Learning using an existing similarity based WSD algorithm (Karov and Edelman, 1998) to annotate a corpus for non-literal language.

Some researchers used *knowledge resources* to strengthen the approaches for metaphor detection. The work in (Gedigian *et al.*, 2006) proposed a technique to detect metaphorical verb usage by utilizing existing knowledge sources such as WordNet® (Fellbaum, 1998), FrameNet (Baker et al., 1998) and PropBank (Kingsbury and Palmer, 2002). Krishnakumaran and Zhu (2007) proposed an approach on the basis of violations in co-occurring noun and verb phrases using WordNet® hierarchies. The works in (Mohler *et al.*, 2013) and (Wilks *et al.*, 2013) also utilized WordNet® ontology for recognizing metaphors. Dunn (2013) proposed a domain interaction system namely Measuring and Identifying Metaphor in Language (MIMIL) using SUMO ontology (Niles and Pease, 2011). The default sense of lexical items in a sentence were mapped to concepts from SUMO ontology on the basis of domain type and event status. Tsvetkov *et al.* (2014) and Bracewell et al. (2014) used the concept of hybrid feature set by using features from WordNet, MRCPD and vector representations. Klebanov *et al.* (2015) evaluated the effect of concreteness as a feature for metaphor detection using MRCPD. Gargett and Branden (2015) proposed using sensory features to enhance the process of metaphor detection using Affective Norms for English Word (ANEW) and MRCPD.

Ferrari (1996) proposed an approach based on the analysis of syntactic patterns and used textual cues such as *metaphorically, figuratively* and *like* to detect metaphors. The works in (Sardinha, 2002; Sardinha, 2006) suggested using corpus-based metrics such as collocations list, word frequency and semantic-distance for metaphor detection. Turney *et al.* (2011) observed that metaphorical usage is directly correlated with the degree of abstractness in a word's contextual usage. They proposed an approach to identify metaphorical verbs and adjectives using an algorithm to calculate abstractness given in (Turney and Littman, 2003). Hovy *et al.* (2013) proposed an approach based on features derived from syntactic patterns and word embeddings (Collobert *et al.*, 2011) to analyze the context of a word usage. They used Support Vector Machine (SVM) classifier with tree kernels to identify metaphorical words.

Strazalkowski *et al.* (2013) utilized topic chaining and imageability score to identify metaphorical usage in text. Neuman *et al.* (2013) developed a rule based approach which combines selectional preference and abstractness of words to identify metaphors. Schulder and Hovy (2014) proposed a statistical domain-independent approach based on a metric term relevance derived from Term Frequency-Inverse Document Frequency (TF-IDF). A term is categorized as metaphor if the domain relevance and common relevance for a given term is lower than a predetermined threshold.

Our work is different from earlier works in terms of improved and rich feature set that we employ. Unlike previous works which used a subset of conceptual features, we utilize a multifarious feature set. Along with that, we introduce different affective features which deal with abstract concepts like mental state, physical state, and behavioral characteristics. We systemically extend the coverage of MRCPD to include unavailable terms rather than taking average values as in (Gargett and Branden, 2015). To the best of our knowledge, CRF for metaphor classification has not yet been fully investigated, especially in the context of large, and overlapping feature set. Hovy *et al.* (2013) compared their proposed approach with CRF. However they did not emphasize on the feature set and relations which can be exploited while using a CRF model.

3 Proposed Methodology

Our methodology is based on an innovative application of CRF on an amalgamation of syntactic, conceptual, affective and word embeddings based features extracted by using corpus and knowledge resources. We now give a detailed description of the features that we have employed, our technique for expanding the coverage of MRCPD using WordNet® and an approach to build a CRF model for *Metaphor Detection*.

3.1 Feature Set

We have built a hybrid feature set drawing upon traditional features as well as on the basis of our inferences from the existing literature that are likely to enhance the process of metaphor detection. The feature set is categorized into four categories namely, Syntactic Feature set, F_S, Conceptual feature set, F_C, Affective feature set, F_A and Contextual feature set, F_X.

3.1.1 Syntactic Features

The set of syntactic features (SF) is defined as a feature vector $F_S = \{F_{S_1}, F_{S_2}, \ldots, F_{S_5}\}$, based on a word attributes, sentence structure and dependency between components of a sentence. We use Stanford CoreNLP (Manning et al., 2014) to extract following syntactic features:

1. *Lemma*: It includes lemmas i.e. the base form, for all tokens in the corpus.
2. *PoS*: It denotes grammatical word-category such as noun, verb etc. for each word in a sentence.
3. *Named_Entity_Type*: It marks named, numerical and temporal entities such as *person, location, money, number, date, time etc.*
4. *Dependency*: It provides information about the position of a word with respect to grammatical structure of a sentence including relations between words and modifiers.
5. *Stop_word*: It marks a word as *content* or *non-content* word, based on a list of stop-words.

3.1.2 Conceptual Features

The set of conceptual features (CF) is defined as a feature vector, $F_C = \{F_{C_1}, F_{C_2}, \ldots, F_{C_5}\}$, which consists of features based on the meaning, abstract attributes of a word and its measured impact on a large corpus. We use MRCPD (Wilson, 1988), a large psycholinguistics database to extract the conceptual features of a word enumerated below (Gilhooly and Logie, 1980; Paivio and Madigan, 1968; Toglia and Battig, 1978). These conceptual features have numerical values ranging from 100 to 700.

1. *Concreteness*: It is a measurement of the ability of a word to refer to concrete concepts.
2. *Familiarity*: It refers to a feeling of knowing the word or concept behind a word, depending upon how commonly the word is used.
3. *Imageability*: It refers to the expressiveness of a word to evoke a visual image of the concept behind the word.
4. *Frequency*: It refers to the frequency of occurrence of a word sense in the Brown corpus.
5. *Meaningfulness*: It is a measure of the association of a given word with other words. We utilize the Colorado based *Meaningfulness* rating, MEANC.

3.1.3 Affective Features

The set of affective features (AF) is defined as a feature vector, $F_A = \{F_{A_1}, F_{A_2}, \ldots, F_{A_5}\}$, based on the affective concepts correlated with an affective word. We use WordNet Affect (Strapparava and Valitutti, 2004) to extract following affective features:

1. *Cognitive_State*: It denotes mental state or feelings such as confusion. Labels *mood, sensation, emotional response* are merged with *cognitive state* label because of very few instances and indirect dependence.
2. *Physical_State*: It refers to physical or bodily state such as illness.
3. *Trait*: It denotes characteristics of personality such as aggressiveness.
4. *Attitude*: The label *behavior* and *attitude* are merged together as they are interrelated.
5. *Emotion*: It refers to emotional state or process such as joy, anger.

3.1.4 Contextual Features

Word Embeddings provide semantic information about a word and are capable of comparing words on basis of relatedness, analogy, coherence and context, the criteria we use for metaphor detection as well. We use word embeddings by Huang et al. (2012) as it captures local i.e. syntactic information as well global context based on word's usage in large corpus. CWE is trained using local context only. Word embeddings are used as contextual features (XF) and represented as a 50 dimensional vector, $F_X = \{F_{X_1}, F_{X_2}, \ldots, F_{X_{50}}\}$.

3.2 Extending MRCPD using WordNet

The MRCPD resource contains linguistic information for over 150,000 words. However, psycholinguistic features are available only for a limited number of words. A total of 8228 words are available for Concreteness rating, 9392 for Familiarity, 9240 for Imageability and 5450 words for Colerado norms based meaningfulness rating (Wilson, 1988). As a result, several words which are used frequently is not available in the database. Liu et al. (2014) proposed extending MRCPD for imageability rating using synonymy and hyponymy relations from WordNet. We strive to use a rich feature set comprising of other features such as concreteness, familiarity and meaningfulness, thus expanding MRCPD for all of these features.

WordNet®(Princeton University, 2010) is an online machine readable lexical database for English language developed by Christiane Fellbaum at Princeton University. In WordNet®, words are grouped on the basis of cognitive concepts known as *synset*, a set of synonymous words. Senses in a synset are arranged in a form of a list on the basis of decreasing frequency count in the Brown corpus (Francis and Kucera, 1979) For example, if we search the word, *man,* we observe that its first sense *<man#1, adult-male#1>* sense has occurred 749 times in the Brown corpus whereas its second sense *<homo#2>* occurred only 29 times. So, we can say, that highest ranked sense is the most frequently used sense for a word. We use this inference to prioritize senses in our technique to extend the coverage of words with psychological features in MRCPD. The hyponymy relation provide a more specific instance for a concept. E.g. for the word, beverage, we obtain {*milk, tea, wish-wash, hydromel, oenomel, soft drink* etc.} as hyponymy concepts. However, *hydromel, oenomel, wish-wash* are relatively less familiar, have lower imageability, and have a lower probability of co-occurrence with other concepts. Therefore, we find it more judicious to consider only synonymy relations from WordNet® while expanding MRCPD.

As an example, consider the word, *deviance* which is not in MRCPD. We extract its synset {*aberrance, aberration, deviation*} from WordNet in order of decreasing Brown frequency. Next, we check the availability of each of these synonyms in MRCPD until a match is found. In this case, the word, *aberration* is available in MRCPD. Therefore, the conceptual features for *aberration* is assigned to *deviance*. Similarly, in case of *courtroom*, the word *court* is selected as a substitute and its conceptual features are extracted.

3.3 Approach

The proposed approach is divided in three phases namely, Data Processing, Feature Extraction and Model Building.

1. Data Processing phase: This involves data cleaning, tokenization and conversion to CoNLL[2] data format. After data processing, we obtain a sequence of tokens derived from sentences of the corpus.

2. Feature Extraction phase: This is sub-divided into four parts: Syntactic Feature Extraction, Conceptual Feature Extraction, Affective features extraction and Contextual feature extraction. The extraction process is explained in subsections 3.1 and 3.2. We use a context window of 7 words i.e. the word itself, 3 previous words and 3 next words, whose features are used to predict the label/class of a token.

3. Model Building phase: CRF (Lafferty *et al.*, 2001) is a probabilistic sequence labelling algorithm which takes an input sequence *X,* and predict the class label, *Y.* Since we are performing binary classification, *Y* consists of only two labels namely {*M, NM*} where *M* stands for metaphor and *NM* for otherwise cases. CRF doesn't make the assumption that features are independent and it is capable of handling large number of inter-independent or over-lapping features unlike joint probability based models such as HMM which becomes intractable in such cases.

In our approach, these dependencies are defined by analyzing their effect on precision and recall. Thus, creating a feature set more aligned towards precise detection of metaphor without compromising recall. Features are defined in a template file (in case of CRF++) along with the context window and inter-dependencies between different features such as concreteness/pos, imageability/concreteness, cognitive_state/concreteness and so on. $X_{1:N}$ is a feature vector which is generated on the basis of a given template file. The joint distribution for the label sequence *Y* given *X* is as in eq. (1):

$$p(y|x,\alpha) = \frac{1}{Z(x)} \exp(\textstyle\sum_k \alpha_k \sum_i^n f(y_{i-1}, y_i, x, i)) \quad (1)$$

Where $f(y_{i-1}, y_i, x, i)$ is a feature/transition function, y_{i-1}, y_i are class labels, x is an input sequence and i is an input position, $Z(x)$ is a Normalization factor and α_k is a parameter vector. The elements of the parameter vector, $\{\alpha_k\} \epsilon R^K$ are calculated from the training data to maximize the likelihood of $p(y|x)$.

[2] CoNLL Data Format: http://ilk.uvt.nl/conll/#dataformat

4 Experiments and Results

We used CRF++ (V0.58) (Kudo, 2005), an open source C++ implementation of CRF based classifier for our experiments and VU Amsterdam Metaphor Corpus as dataset.

4.1 Dataset

We used VU Amsterdam Metaphor corpus (Steen *et al.*, 2010) developed by MIP Pragglejaz group. The annotation for metaphor in a sentence is based on anomaly between basic meaning of the term and contextual meaning of the term in the given sentence (Pragglejaz Group, 2007). The corpus is a small set of BNC Baby manually annotated for metaphors in XML format. For our experimental purpose, we converted the XML dataset into CoNLL format. We have considered words marked with MRW-Met sub-class as *Metaphor* and all other categories as *Non-Metaphor*. In original files, total number of metaphors is 25496, however in few cases we have separated multi-word expressions and marked all of them as Metaphor or Not Metaphor (whichever is the initial case) which led to minor increase in total number of metaphors. We have performed 10-fold cross validation across every genre as well as on overall dataset say Dataset2. The percentage of metaphor in each dataset is given in Table1.

Dataset	M	NM	Total Tokens	% of M
News	8388	52207	60595	13.84
Academic	8416	63275	71691	11.74
Fiction	4883	45105	49988	9.77
Conversation	3854	54342	58196	6.62
Total	25541	214929	240570	10.62
Legends: M: Metaphor, NM: Not Metaphor				

Table1: Dataset

4.2 Experiments

We trained the CRF based classifier on categorized datasets in steps to analyze individual effect of every feature set. During feature extraction, we observed that affective features are too sparse i.e. exists in case of affective words only which is around 11% (refer Table2). Therefore, affective feature set is merged with conceptual feature set to analyze its effect on metaphor detection in an open domain dataset.

Dataset	% of AW	% of AW-M
News	11.34	33.47
Academic	10.93	24.11
Fiction	12.72	22.33
Conv	11.46	16.71
Total	11.53	24.74
Legends: AW: Affective words, M-Metaphor		

Table2: Coverage of Affective Words

However, we observed that 24.74% of total affective words in corpus are annotated as metaphors in dataset indicating a correlation between metaphors and affective words. Below (Table3-7) are the values obtained for accuracy, precision and recall.

Dataset	A	P-M	P-N	R-M	R-N
News	90.62	70.60	93.98	54.94	96.46
Academic	90.58	62.21	90.28	46.37	97.85
Fiction	92.46	67.47	90.60	44.15	98.47
Conv	94.95	65.82	96.40	49.52	97.90
Avg	92.15	66.52	92.82	48.74	97.67
Dataset2	91.80	63.44	92.86	54.55	97.19

Table 3: Metaphor Detection using CRF classifier and Syntactic Feature (SF) set

Dataset	A	P-M	P-N	R-M	R-N
News	91.09	71.09	94.60	59.76	96.44
Academic	90.77	62.06	91.28	51.30	97.64
Fiction	92.67	67.06	91.47	49.00	98.20
Conv	95.15	66.60	96.62	53.79	97.73
Avg	92.42	66.70	93.49	53.46	97.50
Dataset2	92.10	64.32	93.39	58.54	97.27

Table 4: Metaphor Detection using CRF classifier with Conceptual Feature (SF+CF) set

Dataset	A	P-M	P-N	R-M	R-N
News	91.13	71.09	94.73	60.25	96.40
Academic	90.72	61.82	91.23	51.31	97.58
Fiction	92.67	66.86	91.53	49.46	98.16
Conv	95.15	66.60	96.62	53.89	97.70
Avg	92.42	66.59	93.53	53.73	97.46
Dataset2	92.08	64.14	93.46	58.64	97.20

Table 5: Metaphor Detection using CRF classifier with Conceptual Feature and Affective Feature (SF+ CF + AF) set

Dataset	A	P-M	P-N	R-M	R-N
News	90.43	69.24	94.11	55.30	96.16
Academic	90.45	61.04	90.58	48.05	97.80
Fiction	92.45	65.58	90.38	47.93	98.06
Conv	94.96	64.52	96.50	53.32	97.61
Avg	92.07	65.10	92.89	51.15	97.41
Dataset2	91.73	62.20	93.10	56.49	96.88

Table 6: Metaphor Detection using CRF classifier with Contextual Feature (SF + XF) set

Dataset	A	P-M	P-N	R-M	R-N
News	90.90	70.49	94.60	58.86	96.48
Academic	90.57	61.06	91.05	50.87	97.57
Fiction	92.64	66.54	91.22	49.66	98.16
Conv	95.12	65.97	96.60	54.43	97.63
Avg	92.31	66.02	93.37	53.46	97.46
Dataset2	91.97	63.33	93.34	58.71	96.95

Legends: Conv: Conversation; A: Accuracy; P-M: Precision for Metaphor Class; P-N: Precision for Non Metaphor Class; R-M: Recall for Metaphor class and R-N: Recall for Non- Metaphor class; Avg: Average of results across every genre.

Table 7: Metaphor Detection using CRF classifier on Hybrid Feature (SF+CF+AF+XF) set

Analysis: Extension of MRCPD with WordNet led to higher coverage and fewer missing values in conceptual feature vector. From the results in Table 3-4, we observed that inclusion of conceptual features significantly improved recall (up to 5%) for metaphors however it didn't have any visible effect on precision. Due to sparse affective feature vector, we could not observe any major impact on either precision or recall on adding affective feature set (refer Table5). Contextual Features i.e. embeddings with Syntactic features was also effective in recognizing metaphors but did not supersede the feature set {SF+CF} (refer Table4 and Table6). The combination {SF, CF, AF} (refer Table5) and {SF, CF, AF, XF} (refer Table8) didn't show any significant improvement over feature set {SF+CF}.

We gathered that presence of open category words (non-content words) such as determiners, conjunction etc. limited the effect of inter-dependent features. Consider the following sentence (metaphors in bold):

It would be *also necessary 'to* ***smash*** *the* ***decrepit, effete*** constitution that allows a minority to **capture power**, and then **use** it ruthlessly **in** the **interests** of the privileged few'.

Here, *smash* is used metaphorically. Despite of considering a context window of 7 words i.e. *also necessary to* ***smash*** *the decrepit effete,* we were unable to capture object of interest, i.e. *constitution.*

4.3 Comparison

We compared our approach with approaches proposed by Dunn (2013), Klebanov *et al.* (2015) and Hovy *et al.* (2013). Dunn used logistic regression classifier implemented in WEKA (Hall, 2009) on features extracted from SUMO Ontology. Klebanov *et al.* (2015) used concreteness as a feature with baseline features (Klebanov *et al.*, 2014) and optimal weighting technique. The dataset used was VU Amsterdam Metaphor corpus. Hovy *et al.* (2013) used SVMlight Tree Kernel (TK) implementation by (Moschitti, 2006) with syntactic features and CWE. However, they conducted the experiments on their own dataset, say Dataset3.

Model	A	P-M	R-M	F-M	*F-M
Proposed model^	**92.31**	**66.02**	53.46	59.08	77.22
Proposed model^^	91.97	63.33	58.71	**60.93**	**78.02**
Klebanov (2015)**	NA	43.8	**66.9**	51.1	NA
(Dunn, 2013)***	57.26	53.75	39.40	45.47	56.1
Proposed model#	**93.96**	**76.19**	47.42	58.46	77.60
Hovy *et al.*(2013)	75	70	**80**	**75**	NA

Legends: A: Accuracy; P-M: Precision for Metaphor Class; R-M: Recall for Metaphor class ; F-M is F-measure for Metaphor class; *F-M is average F-measure for both classes; NA: Not Available

^average of results obtained in each genre for {SF+CF+AF+XF}

^^results across all genres, *i.e.* Dataset2 for {SF+CF+AF+XF}

**average values for optimal weighting with concreteness measure method recommended in paper

***Results for MRW-Met Sub-Class across all genres

#results on Hovy *et al.*(2013) data *i.e.* Dataset3 using {SF+CF+AF+XF}

Table 8: Comparison of proposed model with previous approaches

By using CRF as a classifier, there is a significant improvement in accuracy and precision in comparison to models used in previous approaches. From Table8, we observed that CRF based classifier with {SF+CF+AF+XF} feature set outperformed approaches proposed by Dunn (2013) and Klebanov *et al.* (2015) in terms of accuracy, precision and F-measure (refer Table8). Klebanov *et al.* (2015) approach was based on optimal weighting to obtain optimal F-score which lead to comparatively higher recall. It is worth noting that accuracy increased by 18.96% and precision by 6.19% with respect to system proposed by Hovy *et al.* (2013). However, Hovy *et al.* (2013) outperformed in terms of recall and F-measure for metaphor class. The problem of low recall is likely to be resolved by optimizing the model for optimal F-measure as in Klebanov *et al.* (2015).

5 Conclusion

We used a CRF based classifier to perform metaphor detection in text. Using a rich feature set and a wide context window, we demonstrated the advantage of using CRF classifier over other classifiers in terms of accuracy and precision. We analyzed the efficacy of using CRF classifier over various combinations of feature sets. We expanded the coverage of the conceptual features of MRCPD using WordNet® ontology, resulting in significant improvement in the recall of metaphor detection. In future, we would like to conduct an in-depth analysis of affective features, fine-tune the process of feature selection and develop a multi-stage model for metaphor processing.

Acknowledgments

We acknowledge the contribution of Yash Kukreti and Ayush Garg in coding and implementation of the paper. We would also like to thank anonymous reviewers for helping us clarify several points and their insightful comments.

References

Baker, Collin F., Charles J. Fillmore, and John B. Lowe. 1998. "The Berkeley framenet project." *Proceedings of the 17th international conference on Computational linguistics-Volume 1*. Association for Computational Linguistics.

Baumer, Eric PS, James P. White, and Bill Tomlinson. 2010. "Comparing semantic role labeling with typed dependency parsing in computational metaphor identification." *Proceedings of the NAACL HLT 2010 Second Workshop on Computational Approaches to Linguistic Creativity*. Association for Computational Linguistics.

Birke, Julia and Anoop Sarkar. 2006. A clustering approach for the nearly unsupervised recognition of nonliteral language. In In Proceedings of EACL-06, pages 329–336.

Birke, Julia, and Anoop Sarkar. 2007. "Active learning for the identification of nonliteral language." *Proceedings of the Workshop on Computational Approaches to Figurative Language*. Association for Computational Linguistics.

Bracewell, David B., Marc T. Tomlinson, Michael Mohler, and Bryan Rink. 2014. "A tiered approach to the recognition of metaphor." In *Computational Linguistics and Intelligent Text Processing*, pp. 403-414. Springer Berlin Heidelberg.

Cameron, Lynne, and Alice Deignan. 2003. "Combining large and small corpora to investigate tuning devices around metaphor in spoken discourse." *Metaphor and Symbol* "18.3 (2003): 149-160.

Christine Fellbaum, editor. 1998. WordNet: An Electronic Lexical Database. MIT Press

Collobert, Ronan, Jason Weston, Léon Bottou, Michael Karlen, Koray Kavukcuoglu, and Pavel Kuksa. 2011. "Natural language processing (almost) from scratch." The Journal of Machine Learning Research 12 (2011): 2493-2537.

Dunn, Jonathan. 2013. "What metaphor identification systems can tell us about metaphor-in-language". In Proceedings of the *First Workshop on Metaphor in NLP*, pages 1–10, Atlanta, Georgia.

Fass. D. 1991. met*: A method for discriminating metonymy and metaphor by computer. Computational Linguistics, 17(1):49–90

Ferrari, Stéphane. 1996. "Using textual clues to improve metaphor processing." Proceedings of the 34th annual meeting on Association for Computational Linguistics. Association for Computational Linguistics.

Francis, W. Nelson, and Henry Kucera. 1979. "Brown corpus manual." Brown University.

Gargett, Andrew, and John Barnden. "Modeling the interaction between sensory and affective meanings for detecting metaphor." *NAACL HLT 2015*(2015): 21.

Gedigan M., J. Bryant, S. Narayanan, and B. Ciric. 2006. Catching metaphors. In Proceedings of the 3rd Workshop on Scalable Natural Language Understanding, pages 41–48, New York

Gibbs, Raymond W. 1984. "Literal Meaning and Psychological Theory*." *Cognitive science* "8.3 (1984): 275-304.

Gilhooly, Kenneth J., and Robert H. Logie. 1980. "Age-of-acquisition, imagery, concreteness, familiarity, and ambiguity measures for 1,944 words." *Behavior Research Methods & Instrumentation* 12.4 (1980): 395-427.

Hall, Mark, Eibe Frank, Geoffrey Holmes, Bernhard Pfahringer, Peter Reutemann, and Ian H. Witten. 2009. "The WEKA data mining software: an update." ACM SIGKDD explorations newsletter 11, no. 1 (2009): 10-18.

Hovy, Dirk, Shashank Srivastava, Sujay Kumar Jauhar, Mrinmaya Sachan, Kartik Goyal, Huiying Li, Whitney Sanders, and Eduard Hovy. 2013. "Identifying metaphorical word use with tree kernels."

In Proceedings of the First Workshop on Metaphor in NLP, pp. 52-57.

Huang, Eric H., Richard Socher, Christopher D. Manning, and Andrew Y. Ng. "Improving word representations via global context and multiple word prototypes." *Proceedings of the 50th Annual Meeting of the Association for Computational Linguistics: Long Papers-Volume 1*. Association for Computational Linguistics, 2012.

Karov, Yael, and Shimon Edelman. 1998. "Similarity-based word sense disambiguation." Computational linguistics 24, no. 1 (1998): 41-59.

Kingsbury, Paul, and Martha Palmer. 2002. "From TreeBank to PropBank."*LREC*.

Klebanov, B.B., Leong, C.W., Heilman, M. and Flor, M., 2014, June. Different texts, same metaphors: Unigrams and beyond. In *Proceedings of the Second Workshop on Metaphor in NLP* (pp. 11-17).

Klebanov, Beata Beigman, Chee Wee Leong, and Michael Flor. "Supervised Word-Level Metaphor Detection: Experiments with Concreteness and Reweighting of Examples." *NAACL HLT 2015* (2015): 11.

Krishnakumaran, S., and X. Zhu. 2007. Hunting elusive metaphors using lexical resources. In Proceedings of the Workshop on Computational Approaches to Figurative Language, pages 13–20, Rochester, NY.

Kudo, Taku. 2005. "CRF++: Yet another CRF toolkit." Software available at http://crfpp.sourceforge.net.

Kudo, Taku, and Yuji Matsumoto. 2005. "YamCha: Yet another multipurpose chunk annotator." *2005-09-05)[2009-02-25]. http://www. chasen. org/~tAKu/software/yamcha.*

Lafferty, John, Andrew McCallum, and Fernando CN Pereira. 2001. "Conditional random fields: Probabilistic models for segmenting and labeling sequence data."

Lakoff, George, and Mark Johnson. 1980. "Metaphors we live by, University of Chicago Press." Chicago, IL.

Liu, Ting, Kit Cho, George Aaron Broadwell, Samira Shaikh, Tomek Strzalkowski, John Lien, Sarah M. Taylor et al. 2014. "Automatic Expansion of the MRC Psycholinguistic Database Imageability Ratings." In *LREC*, pp. 2800-2805.

Manning, Christopher D., Surdeanu, Mihai, Bauer, John, Finkel, Jenny, Bethard, Steven J., and McClosky, David. 2014. The Stanford CoreNLP Natural Language Processing Toolkit. In *Proceedings of 52nd Annual Meeting of the Association for Computational Linguistics: System Demonstrations*, pp. 55-60.

Martin, James H. 1990. A computational model of metaphor interpretation. Academic Press Professional, Inc.

Mason, Zachary J. 2004. "CorMet: a computational, corpus-based conventional metaphor extraction system." Computational Linguistics 30, no. 1 (2004): 23-44.

Mohler, Michael, David Bracewell, David Hinote, and Marc Tomlinson. 2013. "Semantic signatures for example-based linguistic metaphor detection." In Proceedings of the First Workshop on Metaphor in NLP, pp. 27-35.

Moschitti, Alessandro, Daniele Pighin, and Roberto Basili. 2006. "Tree kernel engineering for proposition re-ranking." Proceedings of Mining and Learning with Graphs (MLG 2006).

Neuman, Yair, Dan Assaf, Yohai Cohen, Mark Last, Shlomo Argamon, Newton Howard, and Ophir Frieder. 2013, "Metaphor identification in large texts corpora." e62343.

Niles, Ian, and Adam Pease. 2001. "Towards a standard upper ontology." Proceedings of the international conference on Formal Ontology in Information Systems-Volume 2001. ACM.

Paivio, A., Yuille, J. C. and Madigan, S. A. 1968. Concreteness, imagery and meaningfulness values for 925 words. *Journal of Experimental Psychology Monograph Supplement* 76, (3, Part 2)

Pragglejaz Group. 2007. "MIP: A method for identifying metaphorically used words in discourse." *Metaphor and symbol* 22.1 (2007): 1-39.

Princeton University.2010. "About WordNet." WordNet. Princeton University. http://wordnet.princeton.edu

Rentoumi, Vassiliki, George A. Vouros, Vangelis Karkaletsis, and Amalia Moser. 2012. "Investigating metaphorical language in sentiment analysis: A sense-to-sentiment perspective." ACM Transactions on Speech and Language Processing (TSLP) 9, no. 3 (2012): 6.

Resnik, P. 1993. Selection and Information: A Class-based Approach to Lexical Relationships. Ph.D. thesis, Philadelphia, PA, USA.

Searle, John R. 1985. *Expression and meaning: Studies in the theory of speech acts*. Cambridge University Press.

Sardinha, Tony Berber. 2002. "Metaphor in early applied linguistics writing: A corpus-based analysis of lexis in dissertations." In I Conference on Metaphor in Language and Thought.

Sardinha, Tony Berber. 2006. "Collocation lists as instruments for metaphor detection in corpora." DELTA: Documentação de Estudosem Lingüística Teóricae Aplicada 22, no. 2 (2006): 249-274.

Schulder, Marc, and Eduard Hovy. 2014. "Metaphor detection through term relevance." *ACL 2014* (2014): 18.

Shutova, Ekaterina, Lin Sun, and Anna Korhonen. 2010. "Metaphor identification using verb and noun clustering." *Proceedings of the 23rd International*

Conference on Computational Linguistics. Association for Computational Linguistics.

Steen, G.J., Dorst A.G., Herrmann, J.B., Kaal, A.A.,Krennmayr, T., Pasma, T. 2010. *A method for linguistic metaphor identification. From MIP to MIPVU.*

Strapparava, Carlo, and Alessandro Valitutti. "WordNet Affect: an Affective Extension of WordNet." In *LREC*, vol. 4, pp. 1083-1086. 2004.

Strzalkowski, T., Broadwell, G.A., Taylor, S., Feldman, L., Yamrom, B., Shaikh, S., Liu, T., Cho, K., Boz, U., Cases, I. and Elliott, K., 2013. Robust extraction of metaphors from novel data. In Proceedings of the ACL-13 Workshop on Metaphor (p. 67).

Sutton, Charles, and Andrew McCallum. 2011. "An introduction to conditional random fields." Machine Learning 4, no. 4 (2011): 267-373.

Toglia, Michael P., and William F. Battig. 1978. *Handbook of semantic word norms*. Lawrence Erlbaum.

Tsvetkov, Yulia, Leonid Boytsov, Anatole Gershman, Eric Nyberg, and Chris Dyer. 2014. "Metaphor detection with cross-lingual model transfer."

Turney, Peter D., Yair Neuman, Dan Assaf, and Yohai Cohen. 2011. "Literal and metaphorical sense identification through concrete and abstract context." In Proceedings of the 2011 Conference on the Empirical Methods in Natural Language Processing, pp. 680-690.

Turney, Peter D., and Michael L. Littman. 2003. "Measuring praise and criticism: Inference of semantic orientation from association." *ACM Transactions on Information Systems (TOIS)* 21.4 (2003): 315-346.

Wilks Y. 1978. Making preferences more active. Artificial Intelligence, 11(3):197–223.

Wilks, Yorick, Lucian Galescu, James Allen, and Adam Dalton. 2013. "Automatic metaphor detection using large-scale lexical resources and conventional metaphor extraction." Meta4NLP 2013 (2013): 36.

Wilson, M.D. 1988. The MRC Psycholinguistic Database: Machine Readable Dictionary, Version 2. *Behavioural Research Methods, Instruments and Computers*, 20(1), 6-11.

Token-Level Metaphor Detection using Neural Networks

Erik-Lân Do Dinh[†] **& Iryna Gurevych**[†‡]
[†]Ubiquitous Knowledge Processing Lab (UKP-TUDA)
Department of Computer Science, Technische Universität Darmstadt
[‡]Ubiquitous Knowledge Processing Lab (UKP-DIPF)
German Institute for Educational Research and Educational Information
http://www.ukp.tu-darmstadt.de

Abstract

Automatic metaphor detection usually relies on various features, incorporating e.g. selectional preference violations or concreteness ratings to detect metaphors in text. These features rely on background corpora, hand-coded rules or additional, manually created resources, all specific to the language the system is being used on. We present a novel approach to metaphor detection using a neural network in combination with word embeddings, a method that has already proven to yield promising results for other natural language processing tasks. We show that foregoing manual feature engineering by solely relying on word embeddings trained on large corpora produces comparable results to other systems, while removing the need for additional resources.

1 Introduction

According to Lakoff and Johnson (1980), metaphors are cognitive mappings of concepts from a source to a target domain. While in some works identifying those mappings (*conceptual metaphors*) themselves is the subject of analysis, we concern ourselves with detecting their manifestations in text (*linguistic metaphors*).

Various features have been designed to model either representation of metaphor, prominently e.g. violations of (generalized) selectional preferences in grammatical relations (Wilks, 1978; Shutova, 2013), concreteness ratings to model the difference between source and target concepts (Tsvetkov et al., 2014; Turney and Assaf, 2011), supersenses and hypernym relations (Tsvetkov et al., 2013), or topic models (Heintz et al., 2013; Beigman Klebanov et al., 2014). Some of these features can be obtained in an unsupervised way, but many require additional resources such as concreteness databases or word taxonomies. While this is a good approach for resource-rich languages, this poses problems for languages where such resources are not readily available. Approaches to alleviate this issue often make use of bilingual dictionaries or machine translation (Tsvetkov et al., 2013; Dunn et al., 2014), in itself introducing the need for a new resource resp. introducing a possible new source for misclassification.

In this paper, we present a novel approach for metaphor detection using neural networks on the token-level in running text, relying solely on word embeddings used in context. In recent years, neural networks have been used to solve natural language processing tasks with great effect, but so far have not been applied to metaphor detection. While our approach still has to be tested on data in other languages, it already shows promising results on English data, all the more considering it is not using an elaborate feature set, deriving the representation only from distributed and local context.

We start in Section 2 by discussing previous work on metaphor detection which compares to our work in at least one aspect: granularity of classification, language/resource independence, or the usage of word embeddings. Section 3 details the architecture of our neural network. In Section 4, we describe the used resources and training data and present the results of our method. Concluding this paper, in Section 5 we also give an outlook for future work.

Proceedings of The Fourth Workshop on Metaphor in NLP, pages 28–33,
San Diego, CA, 17 June 2016.

2 Related Work

While some approaches aim at inferring conceptual metaphors, here we mainly discuss works which detect linguistic metaphors, although differing in classification granularity (i.e. detection on token, construction, or sentence level).

Beigman Klebanov et al. (2014) used logistic regression to assess (binary) metaphoricity on the token level, considering only content words. They built upon their work which used unigram, POS, topic model, and concreteness features from a concreteness ratings list, by implementing a reweighing scheme to correct for the imbalanced class distribution in metaphor data (Beigman Klebanov et al., 2015). Re-weighting significantly improved results on their test data, and allows for task-dependent tuning to focus on precision or recall. They also experiment with differences between concreteness ratings in certain grammatical constructions, interpreting the rather small performance increases as an indicator of concreteness possibly not being a defining factor of metaphoricity.

An ensemble approach to detect sentences containing metaphors has been implemented by Dunn et al. (2014). Their system extracts candidate token pairs from parsed text using manually defined syntactic patterns, before applying classifiers—one of them being an overlap classifier for source and target concepts. Employing concreteness ratings it selects the most concrete words related to a given concept, and WordNet for extracting a set of basic semantic categories to which the concepts are mapped. They further use machine translation for concreteness ratings and non-English WordNet-like taxonomies to extend the system to different languages.

Tsvetkov et al. (2013) employed random forests for metaphor detection on adjective-noun constructions. Database-provided features such as concreteness and imageability values are complemented by low-dimensional word embeddings and supersenses. By means of bilingual dictionaries they test their system on datasets in different languages, allowing for the continued use of English resources for feature extraction (e.g. concreteness and imageability databases, WordNet for supersense extraction, etc.).

As an exception to the other discussed systems, Mohler et al. (2014) present a complex system for conceptual metaphor detection, which requires linguistic metaphors identified by a separate system as the input data. For clustering words into conceptual classes, they compare the usage of dependency based vector representations, traditional LSA, and dense word embeddings. Their concept-mapping approach yields significant improvements in accuracy for three languages when using word embeddings; however, for English, LSA produced the best results.

Schulder and Hovy (2014) provide an inherently resource and language independent method by using tf.idf for metaphor detection, requiring only large background corpora and a small set of training sentences. Employing a bootstrapping approach with manually selected seed terms, they achieve rather modest results based on tf.idf alone, but emphasize its potential usefulness as a feature in more advanced multi-feature detection systems.

Closely related, work in metonymy identification also has made use of word embeddings. Among other features commonly used for metaphor detection, such as abstractness or selectional restrictions, Zhang and Gelernter (2015) test different representations of words to detect metonymy using an SVM. To that end they employ word embeddings, LSA, and one-hot-encoding—however, their results do not show clear superiority of one representation over the others.

3 Neural Networks for Metaphor Detection

We propose a neural network approach to metaphor detection in conjunction with word embeddings, i.e. dense vector representations of words. For this purpose, we experiment with multilayer perceptrons (MLP), fully connected feedforward neural networks with an input layer, one or more hidden layers, and an output layer (Figure 1). MLPs have been successfully applied to a variety of standard NLP preprocessing tasks, such as part-of-speech (POS) tagging, chunking, or named entity recognition, but also to more advanced tasks like semantic role labeling (Collobert et al., 2011). In this spirit, we treat metaphor detection as a tagging problem. To that end, we extend and modify a framework for named entity recognition (Reimers et al., 2014),

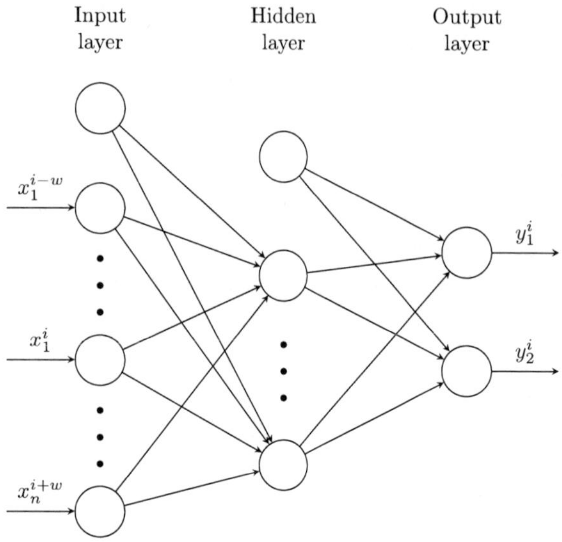

Figure 1: Multilayer perceptron with one hidden layer. Input x for a token at position i is a concatenation of word embedding vectors x^{i-w}, ..., x^{i+w} within a given window w, modeling the local context of the token. The input vector x can be enriched with additional features by concatenating embeddings or numerical values. The output layer uses logistic regression to calculate y_1^i and y_2^i, interpretable as probabilities for metaphorical and literal use of token i.

which is built using the Python deep learning library Theano (Bastien et al., 2012).

The input layer is using a lookup function to extract existing, pre-trained word embeddings for all content words in the data set. More specifically, for each content token, we concatenate the embeddings of the surrounding tokens within a window of $w = 5$ (including non-content tokens, and padded with a randomly created embedding at sentence begin and end), which showed the most promising results in preliminary tests. The rationale of re-using this window approach employed by Collobert et al. (2011) is that, similar to POS tagging on a functional level, context is needed for metaphor detection on a semantic level. We also conduct experiments where we additionally use POS tag embeddings as features, as well as concreteness ratings for comparison purposes. Embeddings/Values for those additional features are appended to the respective word embedding, before concatenating them. We set the hyperbolic tangent as the non-linear activation function in our hidden layer. To prevent overfitting, we employ dropout, which essentially amounts to the creation of several unique neural networks where nodes in the hidden layer are removed at random—those unique networks are averaged over the batches. At test time, the complete network is used. The output layer is implemented as a softmax layer which employs logistic regression to classify a token as being used metaphorically or literally.

We use stochastic gradient descent to train the network, employing negative log-likelihood as the loss function to minimize. In addition to learning the parameters of the hidden and output layer via backpropagation, we also extend that learning to the input (lookup) layer, which allows us to adapt the pre-trained embeddings to the training data. We adjust the learning rate using an annealing schedule, decreasing it linearly with respect to epochs, but keeping it above a set minimum.

The network design thus incorporates various hyper-parameters, of which the following had the largest impact: window size, number of nodes in the hidden layer, initial learning rate (which is gradually lowered to ensure convergence), and mini-batch size (which determines over how many instance vectors the weight updates should be averaged). We use grid search to determine the best performing setting of our network on the validation set(s), and tune it according to the best average performance (F1) over different subcorpora of the used data (Table 1).

Genre	content tokens	met. tokens
academic	36,015	15.6%
conversation	19,807	10.6%
fiction	23,163	14.5%
news	24,880	19.6%
overall	103,865	15.4%

Table 1: Subcorpora of the VU Amsterdam Metaphor Corpus, showing contained content tokens (with POS noun, verb, adjective, adverb), and percentage of metaphorically used tokens.

4 Experiments

For our experiments, we use the pre-trained 300-dimensional word embeddings created with word2vec[1] using the Google News dataset (Mikolov

[1] `https://code.google.com/p/word2vec/`

Genre	B	Token			Token+POS			Token+POS+Conc		
	F1	P	R	F1	P	R	F1	P	R	F1
acprose	.2650	.5791	.5382	.5579	.5775	.5426	.5595	.5841	.5412	**.5618**
convrsn	.2056	.6561	.4863	.5586	.6597	.4941	**.5650**	.6595	.4784	.5545
fiction	.2824	.5597	.4637	.5072	.5703	.4725	**.5168**	.5819	.4527	.5093
news	.3240	.6412	.6293	.6352	.6480	.6293	**.6385**	.6431	.6190	.6308
average	.2735	.6034	.5415	.5707	.6074	.5460	**.5751**	.6110	.5359	.5710
complete	.2703	.5834	.5235	.5518	.5879	.5255	.5550	.5899	.5355	**.5614**

Table 2: Results on the test sets for the tuned neural network. Showing precision (P), recall (R) and F1-measure (F1) regarding metaphorically used tokens, for different feature combinations and VUAMC subcorpora, as well as for the whole corpus (complete). *B* denotes a pseduo-baseline classifying all tokens as metaphorical.

et al., 2013). Training and testing data is taken from the VU Amsterdam Metaphor Corpus (VUAMC) (Steen et al., 2010), a subset of the BNC Baby in which each token is annotated as being used literally or metaphorically. This is done using various fine-grained tags; however, we only use the most clear cut tag *mrw* (metaphor-related word), labeling everything else as literal. Furthermore, because generally only the detection of metaphoricity of content tokens is of interest, we only incorporate labels for tokens having one of the following POS tags (as supplied with the VUAMC): noun, verb, adjective, adverb. Also auxiliary verbs, having lemmas *have*, *be*, or *do*, were filtered out. An overview over the remaining tokens in the subcorpora can be seen in Table 1. The system is trained on each contained genre (*news*, *conversation*, *fiction*, *academic*) separately; for each subcorpus we use a random subset of 76% of the data as a training set, 12% as development set and 12% as test set. We also extend our system to incorporate 10-dimensional POS embeddings, which were initialized randomly and updated over the course of the network's training phase. For comparison, we finally include concreteness values taken from Brysbaert et al. (2014), and train an additional network with it.

The reported inter-annotator agreement for the VUAMC is 0.84 in terms of Fleiss' Kappa—in comparison, treating the gold annotations in the test set (complete) and our system as annotators, we achieve 0.56, indicating room for improvement. More detailed results for our final network as evaluated on the test sets can be seen in Table 2. We observe that extending the word embeddings with the 10-dimensional POS embeddings only has a small influence on the results. Adding the concreteness values does not significantly change the results compared to the token-only based approach, which could be due to several factors. Firstly, the used concreteness values cover only about 80% of the data, with the remaining 20% being assigned a default neutral value. The one-dimensionality of the concreteness feature is also likely to be part of the problem, demanding for a better representation. Last, there is a chance of the word embeddings implicitly capturing the concreteness which needs to be investigated further.

We added a pseudo-baseline (B) where each token is labeled as metaphorical; this is handily beaten by our system. However, more informative is a comparison with the work done by other researchers. Beigman Klebanov et al. (2015) use the same classification granularity for their experiments, but employ cross-validation on 77% of the VUAMC for their evaluation. Still, comparing the results gives an indication of our system's performance. Their best performing feature set shows similar performance on the *academic* dataset, achieving an F1 score of 0.564 compared to 0.558 for our token-only based approach; the *fiction* subcorpus yields 0.493, respectively 0.507. Larger gaps can be observed on the *news* and especially the *conversation* sets, where they report results of 0.590 and 0.396 respectively, compared to our scores of 0.635 and 0.559. The strong performance on the *news* subcorpus can partly be attested to our choice of word embeddings, which were constructed using news texts and thus best capture usage of words in this genre.

We also trained and tested our network on

the complete corpus (*complete*, again using a 76%/12%/12% split), with the results indicating that it generalizes rather well. Looking at the data, we can observe some limitations to our approach. E.g., in the sentence "To throw up an impenetrable Berlin Wall between you and them could be tactless.", "Berlin" and "Wall" are wrongly being tagged as literal, because the used context window is too small to detect their metaphoric usage. Similar problems occur in other cases where insufficient information is available, because of too short sentences, and also at the beginning or end of a sentence, where the vectors are padded with generic embeddings and thus contain less information. Such cases could be treated by using larger parts of text instead of sentences, or by adding topical information gained in unsupervised fashion, as it has been done in related work, e.g. via topic models.

Unique problems arise with classification of tokens in the (often colloquial) *conversation* texts. The sentences in these transcripts are sometimes missing words, have non-grammatical structure, or are wrongly split. For example, consider the sentence, "Yeah, I want a whole with that whole." The only content words are "want", "whole", and "whole", of which the latter two are being wrongly tagged as metaphoric by our system. However, even additional context likely would not improve the classification in this case—because of missing words and incomplete sentences, even humans have a hard time grasping the meaning of this sentence in (textual) context, let alone assessing metaphoricity.

When examining errors by POS tag (Table 3), we note that verbs get misclassified twice as often as nouns, which seems intuitive given that verbs generally are more polysemous than nouns. We can observe increased error rates for tokens that are tagged as being ambiguous between nouns and other POS; considering only these, the percentage of misclassified tokens is double that of the whole noun set. Proper nouns are being tagged as literal by the system in all cases, differing from the gold annotations for just 5 out of 813 instances. However, a metaphoric meaning for 4 of those annotations could be disputed—at least, these annotations are inconsistent with other annotations in the corpus.

Two subclasses of adverbs stand out as yielding substantially higher error rates than the remaining

POS	misclassified	total	percentage
Noun	556	5700	9.75%
Verb	673	3449	19.51%
Adj./Adverb	468	3629	12.90%

Table 3: Number of misclassified tokens in the *complete* test set, detailed by coarse-grained POS tag.

adjectives and adverbs: adverbially used prepositions (e.g. "out" in "carry out"), and borderline cases between adverb and preposition (e.g. "on" in "what's going on"). Arguably these could be considered non-content words and filtered out as well, which would further increase F1 values of our system.

5 Conclusion

We presented a novel approach for supervised metaphor detection, combining pre-trained word embeddings with a neural network architecture. Although we showed that our approach works well with English data, comparing favorably to a state-of-the-art system that employs elaborate features, we still need to examine the performance of our approach on other corpora and different languages, e.g. for historical German data, for which annotated data is still under construction. However, we deem our approach especially suited for this kind of task, as it already shows promising results without any additional features other than basic word embeddings, which can be created in an unsupervised fashion. In future work, we also want to analyze the impact of using genre-specific embeddings, as well as the influence of the training set size on the neural network and its results. Natural next steps also include experiments with more advanced network structures such as Recurrent Neural Networks, specifically Long-Short Term Memory networks (LSTMs).

Acknowledgments

This work has been supported by the Volkswagen Foundation as part of the Lichtenberg-Professorship Program under grant No. I/82806, and by the German Institute for Educational Research (DIPF) as part of the graduate program "Knowledge Discovery in Scientific Literature" (KDSL).

References

Frédéric Bastien, Pascal Lamblin, Razvan Pascanu, James Bergstra, Ian Goodfellow, Arnaud Bergeron, Nicolas Bouchard, David Warde-Farley, and Yoshua Bengio. 2012. Theano: new features and speed improvements. In *Deep Learning and Unsupervised Feature Learning NIPS 2012 Workshop*, pages 1–10, Stateline, NV, USA.

Beata Beigman Klebanov, Chee Wee Leong, Michael Heilman, and Michael Flor. 2014. Different Texts, Same Metaphors: Unigrams and Beyond. In *Proceedings of the Second Workshop on Metaphor in NLP*, pages 11–17, Baltimore, MD, USA. Association for Computational Linguistics.

Beata Beigman Klebanov, Chee Wee Leong, and Michael Flor. 2015. Supervised Word-Level Metaphor Detection: Experiments with Concreteness and Reweighting of Examples. In *Proceedings of the Third Workshop on Metaphor in NLP*, pages 11–20, Denver, CO, USA. Association for Computational Linguistics.

Marc Brysbaert, Amy Beth Warriner, and Victor Kuperman. 2014. Concreteness ratings for 40 thousand generally known English word lemmas. *Behavior Research Methods*, 46(3):904–11.

Ronan Collobert, Jason Weston, Léon Bottou, Michael Karlen, Koray Kavukcuoglu, and Pavel Kuksa. 2011. Natural Language Processing (Almost) from Scratch. *Journal of Machine Learning Research*, 12:2493–2537.

Jonathan Dunn, Jon Beltran de Heredia, Maura Burke, Lisa Gandy, Sergey Kanareykin, Oren Kapah, Matthew Taylor, Dell Hines, Ophir Frieder, David Grossman, Newton Howard, Moshe Koppel, Scott Morris, Andrew Ortony, and Shlomo Argamon. 2014. Language-Independent Ensemble Approaches to Metaphor Identification. In *Workshops at the Twenty-Eighth AAAI Conference on Artificial Intelligence*, pages 6–12.

Ilana Heintz, Ryan Gabbard, Donald S Black, Marjorie Freedman, Ralph Weischedel, and San Diego. 2013. Automatic Extraction of Linguistic Metaphor with LDA Topic Modeling. In *Proceedings of the First Workshop on Metaphor in NLP*, pages 58–66, Atlanta, GA, USA. Association for Computational Linguistics.

George Lakoff and Mark Johnson. 1980. *Metaphors we live by.* University of Chicago Press, Chicago, IL, USA.

Tomas Mikolov, Ilya Sutskever, Kai Chen, Greg Corrado, and Jeffrey Dean. 2013. Distributed Representations of Words and Phrases and their Compositionality. In *Proceedings of NIPS*, pages 1–9, Stateline, NV, USA.

Michael Mohler, Bryan Rink, David Bracewell, and Marc Tomlinson. 2014. A Novel Distributional Approach to Multilingual Conceptual Metaphor Recognition. In *Proceedings of COLING 2014, the 25th International Conference on Computational Linguistics: Technical Papers*, number 2, pages 1752–1763.

Nils Reimers, Judith Eckle-Kohler, Carsten Schnober, Jungi Kim, and Iryna Gurevych. 2014. GermEval-2014: Nested Named Entity Recognition with Neural Networks. In *Workshop Proceedings of the 12th Edition of the KONVENS Conference*, pages 117–120, Hildesheim, Germany. Universitätsverlag Hildesheim.

Marc Schulder and Eduard Hovy. 2014. Metaphor Detection through Term Relevance. In *Proceedings of the Second Workshop on Metaphor in NLP*, pages 18–26, Baltimore, MD, USA. Association for Computational Linguistics.

Ekaterina Shutova. 2013. Metaphor Identification as Interpretation. In *Proceedings of *SEM*, pages 276–285, Atlanta, GA, USA. Association for Computational Linguistics.

Gerard J. Steen, Aletta G. Dorst, J. Berenike Herrmann, Anna Kaal, Tina Krennmayr, and Trijntje Pasma. 2010. *A Method for Linguistic Metaphor Identification. From MIP to MIPVU.* John Benjamins, Amsterdam.

Yulia Tsvetkov, Elena Mukomel, and Anatole Gershman. 2013. Cross-Lingual Metaphor Detection Using Common Semantic Features. In *Proceedings of the First Workshop on Metaphor in NLP*, pages 45–51, Atlanta, GA, USA. Association for Computational Linguistics.

Yulia Tsvetkov, Leonid Boytsov, Anatole Gershman, Eric Nyberg, and Chris Dyer. 2014. Metaphor Detection with Cross-Lingual Model Transfer. In *Proceedings of the 52nd Annual Meeting of the Association for Computational Linguistics*, pages 248–258, Stroudsburg, PA, USA. Association for Computational Linguistics.

Peter D Turney and Dan Assaf. 2011. Literal and Metaphorical Sense Identification through Concrete and Abstract Context. In *Proceedings of the Conference on Empirical Methods in Natural Language Processing*, pages 680–690, Edinburgh, United Kingdom. Association for Computational Linguistics.

Yorick Wilks. 1978. Making Preferences More Active. *Artificial Intelligence*, 11(3):197–223.

Wei Zhang and Judith Gelernter. 2015. Exploring Metaphorical Senses and Word Representations for Identifying Metonyms. *http://arxiv.org/abs/1508.04515.*

Round Up The Usual Suspects: Knowledge-Based Metaphor Generation

Tony Veale
School of Computer Science
University College Dublin
Belfield, Dublin D4, Ireland.
Tony.Veale@UCD.ie

Abstract

The elasticity of metaphor as a communication strategy has spurred philosophers to question its ability to mean anything at all. If a metaphor can elicit different responses from different people in varying contexts, how can one say it has a *single* meaning? Davidson has argued that metaphors have no *special* or *secondary* meaning, and must thus mean exactly what they seem to mean on the surface. It is this literally anomalous meaning that directs us to the pragmatic inferences that a speaker actually wishes us to explore. Conveniently, this *laissez faire* strategy assumes that metaphors are crafted from apt knowledge by speakers with real communicative intent, allowing useful inference to be extracted from their words. But this assumption is not valid in the case of many machine-generated metaphors that merely echo the linguistic form – but lack the actual substance – of real metaphors. We present here an open public resource with which a metaphor-generation system can give its figurative efforts real meaning.

1 The Dreamwork of Language

Metaphor is the rubber cement of language. Not only does it help us to the plug holes on our lexica, we also use it to fill the gaps in our understanding and to hide the cracks in our arguments. For unlike the brittle plaster of literal language, metaphors are elastic and can readily expand to fit our meanings in a shifting conversational context. This elasticity comes at a price, though one which a master orator is happy to pay: our metaphors are elastic because they are indeterminate, underspecified and vague. Like dreams, our metaphors paint vivid pictures with words, albeit with fuzzy and ill-defined edges. Like dreams, metaphors can be highly suggestive, yet leave us feeling confused and uncertain.

If metaphorical images are crisp at their focal points but hazy and dreamlike at their edges, just what is the meaning of any metaphor? The philosopher Donald Davidson (1978) has controversially argued that, like our dreams, our metaphors do not have well-defined meanings, at least not of a kind that an AI researcher, semanticist or computational linguist could squeeze into a symbolic structure. Rather, metaphors can move us to think and feel in certain ways, and perhaps act in certain ways, but like dreams, two analysts (a Jungian and a Freudian, say) can hold conflicting views as to how they should be interpreted and as to what they actually "mean", if anything. So, for Davidson, a metaphor means just what it purports to mean on the surface, that is, what the literal or dictionary senses of its words suggest that it means. This *meaning* is to be distinguished from the panoply of inferences and insights that might later emerge from a metaphor, for regardless of how salient these may seem, they *cannot* be considered its definitive meaning. Freud once joked that when it comes to dreams, a cigar is often just a cigar. For Davidson, a figurative cigar is *always* a cigar, even if the metaphor spurs us to further inference far beyond the realm of tobacco.

If all metaphors mean simply what they seem to mean on the surface, and most – from the very best to the truly awful – are superficially anomalous, how can we tell the good from the bad by simply looking? Indeed, how can we tell *real* metaphors from *fake* metaphors based only on the words they use and their senses in the dictionary? Empirical results seem to bear out Davidson's intuitions regarding our folk grasp of metaphors. Veale (2015)

Proceedings of The Fourth Workshop on Metaphor in NLP, pages 34–41,
San Diego, CA, 17 June 2016. ©2016 Association for Computational Linguistics

reports on experiments in which the outputs of two automated generators of metaphors are compared and contrasted. The first, *@metaphorminute* (from noted Twitterbot builder Darius Kazemi) simply fills the copula template "*A is a B: X and Y*" with more-or-less random word choices for the tenor A, the vehicle B and putative grounds X and Y. The second, *@MetaphorMagnet* (Veale *et al.*, 2015) uses a knowledge-base of stereotypical properties and norms to generate comparisons grounded in a high-degree of similarity *and* semantic tension. In a crowd-sourced evaluation of both, test subjects were asked to rate the perceived comprehensibility of metaphors sampled from each generator. While 75% of *@MetaphorMagnet*'s outputs were said to have medium-high to very-high understandability, over half of *@metaphorminute*'s random offerings were rated just as comprehensible. In fact, because the latter were unconstrained by any representation of knowledge or meaning, subjects rated them as *more* novel than the knowledge-driven metaphors of *@MetaphorMagnet*. Only when subjects were asked to complete partial metaphors in a *cloze* test, to show a real understanding of the author's intent, was the impact of knowledge, meaning and intent made clear: test subjects were able to reconstitute *@MetaphorMagnet*'s outputs with medium-high to very-high confidence in 78% of cases, but were unable to complete the original *@metaphorminute* metaphors with better than random performance.

Davidson's *laissez-faire* take on meaning in metaphor can only take machines so far, and if we want a generator to spark the expected inferences in readers, we must assume a computational notion of meaning that goes deeper than the literal surface. For if we want our automatic generators to achieve more than the mere appearance of comprehensibility and forcefully make their points via metaphor, we must first give them knowledge of the world in which to anchor the insights conveyed by their metaphors. While this is a *big ask* that cannot be realized with any single knowledge-base, we present here a solid open-source foundation for the development of a figurative knowledge system. This knowledge-base, named *the NOC List* (*Non-Official Characterization list*) is a source of stereotypical knowledge regarding popular culture, famous people (real and fictional) and their trademark qualities, behaviours and settings. We show here how this modular resource, designed to grow and evolve, can be used for metaphor generation.

2 The Representational Core of Metaphor

Despite Davidson's withering views on the *hidden* meaning of metaphor, and also, in part, *because* of his radical skepticism, it seems necessary for an AI system to find common ground between the literal or surface meaning of a metaphor and its eventual interpretation in the mind of a listener, since an understanding of one is needed for an appreciation of the other. As such, most symbolic approaches to metaphor interpretation assume that these surface and deep meanings *must* overlap in some representational form, for it is this overlap that allows an NLP system to find its way from one to the other.

Many systems assume that this overlap is *taxonomic* in nature: simply, that the concepts used in the surface meaning share a general categorization with their figurative counterparts. Thus, *gasoline* and *beer* are both liquids, *to drink* and *to run on* are both modes of *consumption*, while *job* and *jail* can each denote a *confining, oppressive situation.* The taxonomic approach actually dates all the way back to Aristotle, but is exemplified by AI models such as those of Wilks (1978), Way (1991) and Fass (1991) and by the psychological theories of Glucksberg (1998). In approaches based on analogy, this shared representation comes in the form of isomorphic aspects of the source and target that are built from identical semantic primitives. Winston (1980), for example, as well as Carbonell (1981), Gentner (1983), Gentner *et al.* (1989), Holyoak & Thagard (1989) and Veale & Keane (1997) all propose AI models that identify a common core of structure shared by the *source* (what Davidson calls the surface meaning) and the *target* (a meaning structure of practical AI merit whose existence Davidson denies on philosophical grounds). Other symbolic approaches employ a liberal mix of the taxonomic and the analogical, from that of Hobbs (1981) to Martin (1990) to Veale (2015). Statistical approaches such as that of Mason (2004) and Shutova (2010a,b), which aim to find metaphors or to find paraphrases for metaphors that use more conventional (if not always literal) terms, avoid the thorny issue of deep meaning by remaining resolutely at the surface and by *not* building an explicit model of meaning. Nonetheless, such approaches tacitly assume the intended meaning *must* share a strong overlap with the surface meaning of its paraphrase. In the following sections we aim to craft an explicit representation for this shared meaning.

3 Persons of Interest: Good, Bad and Ugly

The *Aristotle* system of Veale & Hao (2007) is an online generator of metaphors that allows its users to select a target idea and a property to emphasize. In response, it suggests a range of source ideas that exemplify this property (such as *wolf* for *predatory*, *tiger* for *fierce*, *peacock* for *proud*, and so on), and allows the user to explore the further ramifications of any given choice (e.g. to say that one is *as predatory as a wolf* may suggest that one is *sly* and *lonely* too). *Aristotle* can also go to the Web in real time to tackle the problem of the "unknown tenor," which is to say whenever it lacks knowledge of a target. Thus, given the metaphor *Donald Trump is a thug*, it uses its stereotypical knowledge of *thugs* to hypothesize that *Donald Trump* may be *burly*, *rude*, *brutal*, *gruff* or *sadistic*, and dispatches Web queries to quantify the validity of each hypothesis.

The current work represents a complementary approach to the problem of metaphor generation. Rather than create knowledge representations of generic animals, people or things (such as *wolves*, *thugs* and *insults*) we set out to build a knowledge base of famous proper-named individuals such as *Donald Trump*, *Tony Stark* and *Steve Jobs*. These stereotypes can then be used to construct nuanced similes, metaphors and blends, provided that we imbue our knowledge base (aka the *NOC*) with a rich enough set of *Lego*-like blocks to build its creations. Thus, as we'll see, a system can use the NOC to generate XYZ metaphors such as "*Bruce Wayne is the Donald Trump of Gotham City*."

What makes a person worthy of representation in this knowledge-base, and which aspects of each person should we actually represent? In his 1986 book *The Frenzy of Renown: Fame & its History*, Leo Braudy suggests that fame emerges from "the interplay between the common and the unique in human nature." So the qualities that make a person worthy of figurative comparison are exactly those that seem to exist in a concentrated and quite exemplary form in that one person, yet which are so common in our experience as to be predicated of many. Our ambitions for this representation thus go much farther than that of the *Aristotle* system: we set out to represent not just the simple qualities of an iconic person (those that can be expressed as adjectives) but their many affordances as complex, fully-realized entities situated in the world, such as gender (*male* or *female*), locale (e.g. *New York*, *Gotham City*), style of dress, spouses and known enemies, apt vehicles, apt weapons, domains (e.g., *science, politics*), taxonomic categories (e.g. *Politician*), fictive status (*real* or *fictional*), genres and creators (if fictive), typical activities (e.g., *running political campaigns, building casinos*), political leanings (*left*, *right* or *moderate*) and affiliations (e.g. *Eliot Ness* belongs to *The Untouchables*, *Tony Stark* to *The Avengers*, *Darth Vader* to the *Dark Side*, *Dick Cheney* to the *Republican Party*, etc.). In addition, we divide the adjectival qualities of each person in the NOC into their positive and negative "talking points," the former being qualities with a positive lexical affect, such as *resolute*, *wealthy*, *agile* or *media-savvy*, the latter having an obvious negative affect, such as *evil*, *tight-fisted*, *ingratiating* or *devious*. We strive to provide at least three positive and three negative qualities for each of the 800 persons of interest in the NOC, so that any metaphors or blends built from these stereotypes will be more than one-note clichés, and allow for novelty, nuance and emergent inferences.

We use a conventional AI *frame* format for this knowledge: a frame for each person in the NOC, with its various slots and fillers as outlined above, and a frame for any of those filler concepts that are themselves worthy of further elaboration. Thus, for instance, we define frames for a person's clothing, weapon and vehicle of choice, with slots indicating how each is to be used (e.g. one stabs with a knife, one drives a Mercedes but sails on a yacht, and one wears a hat on one's head but wears shoes on one's feet). One's typical activities are associated with default locations (e.g. one *shops for shoes* in a *shopping mall* but *devises evil schemes* in an *underground lair*), while one's taxonomic categories are themselves organized into a global ontology. A frame system such as this can be organized as a set of semantic triples (much like any semantic network), but we eschew the formalism of semantic Web technologies such as RDFS and OWL for the simplicity of spreadsheets, in which rows represent frames, columns represent slots and cells hold fillers for the corresponding frame slot. We do this to ensure that the NOC is easily shared and modified in an open and cumulative fashion. The NOC can thus be downloaded as a set of spreadsheets, containing approx. 30,000 triples in all, from the site *BestOfBotWorlds.com*. In the following section we show how the knowledge in these spreadsheets can be exploited in the service of metaphor generation.

4 Action figures in their original packaging

It may help to think of the collected personalities and paraphernalia of the NOC as a large toy-box, filled with action figures and their accessories. Our goal is to create a knowledge-base that will allow our machines the freedom to play with combinatorial possibilities much as children play with their toys. Kids show a genuinely ecumenical zeal when playing with action figures, and will happily mix characters of different genres and movie franchises (and even mix figures of very different sizes) when letting their imaginations roam freely. Kids also show little respect for orthodoxy when combining the paraphernalia of one toy genre (G.I. Joe trucks say) with the figures of another (their Harry Potter and Star Wars characters, say). We aim to give our generators of metaphors and blends the same freedom to mix and match in *their* conceptual games.

We decide on which figures to put in our figurative toy box by looking to the Web for insight, specifically to identify those personalities that are frequently used as a source of figurative comparisons. As shown in Veale (2014), the Web is replete with XYZ comparisons of the form "X is the Y of Z" where Y is a proper-named individual that is used to figuratively name a whole class of people. Examples include "red meat is the Donald Trump of cancer" (in which we infer that red meat is asserted to be an *aggressive builder* of cancers) and "the potato is the Tom Hanks of the vegetable world" (which seems to assert that potatoes are as versatile, *qua* ingredient, as Hanks is as an actor). We harvest a large body of these figurative XYZs from the Web, using the telltale capitalization of the Y field to find those that pivot around people. We observe that the use of Y's obeys a power-law distribution, so a small number of popular Y's hog the limelight, such as *Michael Jordan* (an icon of sporting supremacy) and *Chuck Norris* (an icon of rugged simplicity) while the bulk line up to form a long tail of names with fast-descending frequency. We take these Y's as our starting point, and round out the list by including their various spouses, enemies, creators and so on if these are also relevant.

Though one might attempt to use information extraction techniques to automatically populate the fields of the NOC for this large set of Ys, we prefer to fill these fields manually, to build a reusable resource of the highest quality for metaphor generation. It is to this generation task that we turn next.

5 Metaphors as Memes, Tropes and Tweets

The NOC is designed to support the same level of whimsy as one might find in a child's playground, and Twitter proves itself an ideal medium for our systems' whimsical outputs. Limiting its outputs to just 140-character each forces a system to focus on a single central conceit and a pithy framing device. In keeping with human emanations from Twitter, these automated outputs need be neither sober nor profound, and can put the NOC to rather flip uses. Consider this simple framing device, which paints a Nietzschean maxim with colours from the NOC:

> If what doesn't kill you makes you stronger, shouldn't being overwhelmed with ruthless ambition by #HillaryClinton make you more driven?
>
> If what doesn't kill you makes you stronger, shouldn't being knocked out with an Oscar statuette by #DanielDayLewis make you more talented?

Each tweet plugs fillers from a single NOC entry into the same frame. Though no comparison is explicitly made between people, Nietzsche himself is implicitly party to the wry contrast that *is* drawn, for these tweets undercut Nietzsche's aphorism by instantiating it in a way that is both apt *and* goofy.

Many more pieces of "stock wisdom" circulate on Twitter as empty platitudes that are just as ripe for satire using the NOC. Consider these exploits:

> If clothes maketh the woman, would wearing #HillaryClinton's pant suit make you more ambitious? Or more grasping?
>
> Nobody's perfect! My grandpa says to never judge a shallow diarist like #CarrieBradshaw until you've walked a mile in her Manolo Blahniks.

These framing devices are whimsical and fun but a system fails to get out of them anything more than it must put *into* them from the NOC. These single-scope tweets fail to leverage the protean capability of metaphor to spark new meanings at the overlap of ideas plucked from two very different domains. Yet it is a simple matter to choose a framing device that forces individuals with conflicting qualities into a juxtaposition that is at once a meaningful comparison and a sharp contrast. Consider the following tweets which again use a popular frame:

I see myself as capable, but my boss says that I make even someone as incompetent as #EdWood look like #HillaryClinton.

I see myself as insightful, but my friends say that I make even someone as ignorant as #Borat look like #AdamSmith.

This framing device simply chooses two figures from the NOC that are linked by an antonymous quality: *capable* for *Hillary Clinton* (and thus *inept* for *Ed Wood*) and *knowledgeable* for *Adam Smith* (and so *ignorant* for *Borat*). The NOC distribution includes a mapping of talking points to their opposites, which is largely derived from the antonym relationships found in WordNet (Fellbaum, 1998). Let's consider some XYZ metaphors in tweet-form that are also generated using the contents of NOC:

What if #TheEmpireStrikesBack were real? #HillaryClinton could be its #PrincessLeia: driven yet bossy, and controversial too

What if #TheNewTestament were about #AmericanPolitics? #MonicaLewinsky could be its #Lucifer: seductive yet power-hungry, and ruined too.

These XYZ framing devices simply juxtapose two figures from the NOC that share a pair of talking points, preferably one positive and one negative. In the first case, figures are chosen from the realms of the real and the fictional, to allow one to be positioned as a real-world incarnation of the other. These frames share the general linguistic structure used by *@metaphorminute*, though the metaphors here are real, as they are predicated on a sharing of iconic qualities that the system knows to be apt.

Nonetheless, while two shared qualities anchor both of the above metaphors, each tweet actually raises *three* talking points. The additional quality – *controversial* for *Hillary/Leia* and *ruined* for *Monica/Lucifer* – is plucked at random from the talking points of the second input figure (*Hillary* or *Lucifer*) with no regard at all as to its salience to the first (*Leia* or *Monica*). Each tweet thus claims that this third quality is just as salient as the two that are known to be shared, spurring readers to reconcile this extra quality with their own knowledge. In effect, the two shared qualities act as a guarantor of the third, eliciting a good faith response from the reader. So note how the XYZ generator goes confidently out on a limb in these two metaphors:

#NikolaTesla is the real world's #BruceBanner: brilliant and smart, but reclusive

What if #BackToTheFuture were real? #NikolaTesla could be its #DocEmmettBrown: experimental yet nutty, and tragic too

The above tweets, each revolving around the real life figure *Nikola Tesla*, show how a third speculative quality is boldly smuggled into the target domain in plain sight, via a comparison justified by just two shared qualities. Yet in each case this extra quality can be accepted as apt, perhaps even as insightful, in its new context. Tesla was notoriously reclusive, but this can make sense for Banner too, given his fear of public carnage. Tesla also had a tragic end, in large part caused by a surfeit of ideas and a deficit of business sense. Though we cannot know how Doc Brown will end his days, a similar end seems just as conceivable, so the possibility is more thought-provoking than random. If a metaphor generator uses its knowledge in such a way as to meet its readers halfway, its readers will use their imaginations to bridge the remaining gap.

Given that two figures openly share a pair of talking points, a system may introduce a third person rather than a third quality, as in the following:

If #MonicaLewinsky is #Lucifer in a stained blue dress, who in #TheNewTestament is #HillaryClinton most like?

So the connectedness of knowledge in the NOC – essentially a dense semantic-network – allows a system to mine the same seam in multiple tweets. Here it uses the *known enemies* field of the NOC to link *Lewinsky* to *Clinton* and draw the latter into the metaphor, while also accessorizing the tweet with salient material from the former's wardrobe. Just as there can be three people in a marriage, we can also put three in a metaphor, to form a blend:

#LexLuthor combines the best of #WarrenBuffett and the worst of #LordVoldemort: He is rich and successful yet also evil, hateful and bald

This two-way sharing allows anyone to be disintegrated into those facets it shares with others, so as to be *re-integrated* into an illuminating whole via blending. And though metaphors are asymmetric, we cannot help but see shades of *Lex Luthor* in the market success of *Warren Buffett*, the famed sage of Omaha, making Luthor the sage of Metropolis.

6 Strange Dreams Are Made of This

Davidson's likening of metaphors to dreams was motivated by more than a desire to show that the "true" meaning of metaphors is just as tendentious a notion as the "true" meaning of dreams. Metaphors, like dreams, slip the surly bonds of commonsense semantics to explore areas of the imagination that challenge, even defy, literal expression. In fact, metaphor is often seen as being the engine of much of what is curious and creative in dreams, and any generative system that aims to flex its imagination should first show a mastery of metaphor.

Many dreams revolve around conflict – arising from a desire for wish-fulfillment and discord resolution – and the NOC allows a system to imagine conflict between iconic figures. Freud (1933) saw dreams as the royal road to the unconscious, so these conflicts must suggest real symbolic insights. A system must thus invent both a dream metaphor *and* its meaning, that is, its Freudian interpretation:

> I dreamt I was paying kickbacks to the police chief with #MayorJoeQuimby when we were cut with a Jedi lightsaber by #LukeSkywalker

> I guess #LukeSkywalker and #MayorJoeQuimby represent warring parts of my personality: the honest vs. corrupt sides. #Honest=#Corrupt

As shown above, the NOC is used to invent a conflict between two iconic figures, blending a typical activity of one with an assault with an apt weapon from another. The domain-crossed actors are chosen because they exhibit conflicting qualities (e.g. *honest* vs. *corrupt*) and it is this conflict that yields the psychological motivation – and the meaning – of a dream. Here is another pair of example tweets:

> I dreamt I was holding evasive press conferences with #DonaldRumsfeld when we were pierced with a sharpened chop stick by #AungSanSuuKyi

> I guess #AungSanSuuKyi and #DonaldRumsfeld represent warring parts of my personality: the caring vs. uncaring sides. #Caring=#Uncaring

For comparison, let us try and build a generator of dreams that does not use the NOC but which relies instead on a more conventional font of knowledge about dreams: the so-called *dream dictionary*. The Web (as well as countless books) is a source of the standard interpretations of a many dream symbols, and we harvest 5000 or so of these with a web spider from the popular site www.dreammoods.com. The following pair of tweets hinges on the symbol Reunion: the first sets the scene, the second makes wholesale reuse of the "dictionary" interpretation:

> Last night I dreamt I was a soldier, attending a reunion. What does this mean? #Reunion

> Well, to dream that you are attending a reunion suggests that there are feelings from the past which you need to acknowledge and recognize.

These dreams are only partially machine-generated then, combining a scene-setting tweet that is wholly invented with a response that is human-crafted. The first tweet in each pair simply takes a triple from a knowledge-base of norms – e.g. *soldiers attend reunions* – whose agent or whose object is a match for the dream symbol. In this next example, the dream symbol matches the agent of the triple:

> Last night I dreamt I was a reporter, conducting inquiries. What does this mean? #Reporter

> Well, to dream that you are a newspaper reporter indicates that you are making a conscious and objective observation of your life. #Reporter

These half-machine/half-human inventions do not use the NOC, and exchange celebrity casting for a psychoanalytical insight that, though perhaps just psychobabble, carries the ring of real folk wisdom. It is an interesting question, then, as to whether we humans see greater merit in these half-human creations than in fully machine-crafted NOC creations. The world has little need of an artificial generator of ersatz dreams, of course, yet if metaphor really is the dreamwork of language as Davidson suggests, a marked preference for machine "dreams" would offer a clear vote in support of a computer's ability to craft its own metaphors *and* meanings.

7 To Tweet, Perchance to Dream

We turn to volunteers on the crowd-sourcing platform *CrowdFlower.com* to quantify the relative merit of each kind of dream metaphor and its interpretation. We paid these volunteers a small sum to provide their ratings of the *interestingness* of each dream scenario (the first tweet in a pair), the *insightfulness* of the offered interpretation (in the second tweet of a pair), and the *symbolic richness* of a dream, regardless of whether one agrees with the interpretation or not (so, both tweets together). We sampled 30 *dream+interpretation* tweet pairs of each kind from the outputs of their respective generators, and elicited ten ratings for each, along each of the 3 dimensions listed above. Judges were filtered for scammer-like non-engagement using the usual tests, and were asked to rate each dimension on a five-point scale (via radio buttons) ranging from *Not At All* (1) to *Very Much So* (5). The average human ratings for each dimension for each kind of dream generation is presented in Table 1.

Strategy→ *↓Dimension*	*NOC dreams, interpretations*	*dream dictionary interpretations*
Interestingness	**3.35 ± 0.38**	2.93 ± 0.42
Insightfulness	3.22 ± 0.34	**3.24 ± 0.37**
Symbolism	3.12 ± 0.35	**3.17 ± 0.36**
All dimensions	**3.23 ± 0.37**	3.11 ± 0.41

Table 1. *Average human ratings for dreams of both types, with their interpretations, on three dimensions (and the average of all three together).*

It appears human raters judge the NOC dreams as more interesting than the corresponding non-NOC scenarios, though raters also judged interpretations for the latter (which are taken wholesale from human-crafted dream dictionaries) as ever-so-slightly more insightful than the NOC-derived alternatives. These stock psychological interpretations are also judged to make deeper use of dream symbols than their NOC counterparts. Nonetheless, only the difference in *interestingness* proves to be statistically significant (using the Wilcoxon signed-rank test), and the average of all 3 dimension taken together also favors the NOC tweets over their competition.

Ultimately, this is a small-scale evaluation of what is little more than a toy-box test of the NOC as a resource for meaningful metaphor generation. Yet we anticipate that the NOC and its many affordances – which will surely grow given the open status of the resource – will lend itself to many more uses of automated metaphor generation, in systems of varying ambition and complexity, from playful bots to quirky games to serious research.

8 Conclusions

Computational metaphor generation is a task that aims to replicate a measure of human creativity with language, and as such, it belongs squarely to the field of *Computational Creativity* (or CC; see Veale, 2012). But as a discipline, CC does not distinguish itself from other branches of AI / NLP by its use of distinctive algorithms or particular data structures. Rather, CC is an AI sub-discipline best characterized by its philosophy, especially as it pertains to automated generation. CC systems each explore their own conceptual space of generative possibilities, as defined either by explicit axioms or by the procedural semantics implicit in their code. Though a CC system may encounter many well-formed possibilities when exploring a space, it can weigh and evaluate only a small number of these possibilities. A creative system must be more than a *mere generator* of well-formed outputs; it must be a selective producer that uses knowledge – of a domain and a target audience – to select, rank and filter possibilities, to generate products that it itself appreciates as interesting, useful and novel.

The limits of a system's knowledge determine the limits of what it can perceive and conceive, and thus the limits of what it can appreciate in its own outputs. But as yet, just as CC has no unique algorithms or data structures to call its own, it has few knowledge sources of any real scale that can be openly shared and reused. This paper has presented a new public resource, which – though still in its early stages of development – can be shared and reused by AI researchers to build systems that squeeze novelty and value from familiar ideas. We have motivated this resource via the difficult task of *metaphor generation*, showing how AI/CC/NLP systems can use this rich symbolic knowledge to ground the meaning of their own creative outputs. Computer-generated metaphors that are insightful, interesting and resonant in their use of symbols will find many applications, from entertainment to education to the pure whimsy of the following (via a Twitterbot that makes full use of the NOC):

> Hulk hate puny humans who tweet about starring in reality TV shows. Hulk smash #KimKardashian and the Rolls Royce she rode in on!

We are on more serious ground when we suggest that automatic generation will allow researchers to test metaphor theories in a constructive fashion, by building robust proofs of concept, and will allow for the creation of artificial experimental stimuli. We hope that the NOC – and other resources that build upon it – will allow researchers to explore the computational possibilities of metaphor generation with the same ease, and scale of ambition, with which they now explore automated analysis. This truly is the dream work of language research.

Acknowledgements

The author is grateful to the European Commission for funding this work via the WHIM project (What If Machine; grant number 611560) and the PROSECCO project (grant number 600653). The author is also grateful for the support of Science Foundation Ireland (SFI) via the ADAPT *Centre for Global Intelligent Content*. and for the assistance of Alessandro Valitutti with the experiments reported in section 7. The various elements of the NOC resource can be downloaded from the Web from the website *BestOfBotWorlds.com*

References

Carbonell, J. G. (1981). Metaphor: An inescapable phenomenon in natural language comprehension. *Report 2404*. Pittsburgh, PA. Carnegie Mellon Computer Science Dept.

Davidson, D. (1978). What Metaphors Mean. *Critical Inquiry (Special Issue on Metaphor)*, 5(5): 31–47.

Fass, D. (1991). met*: A Method for Discriminating Metonymy and Metaphor by Computer. *Computational Linguistics* 17(1):49–90.

Fellbaum, C. (ed.) (1998) *WordNet: An Electronic Lexical Database* (ISBN: 0-262-06197-X). Cambridge, MA: MIT Press.

Freud, S. (1933). *New Introductory Lectures on Psychoanalysis*. London, UK: Penguin Freud Library 2.

Gentner, D., Falkenhainer, B. and Skorstad, J. (1989). Metaphor: The Good, The Bad and the Ugly. In *Theoretical Issues in NLP*, Yorick Wilks (Ed.) Hillsdale, NJ: Lawrence Erlbaum Associates.

Glucksberg, S. (1998). Understanding metaphors. *Current Directions in Psychological Science,* 7:39-43.

Hobbs, J. (1981). Metaphor Interpretation As Selective Inferencing. In *Proceedings of IJCAI'81, the 7th International Joint Conference on Artificial Intelligence*, Vancouver, BC, Canada, vol. 1:85–91.

Holyoak, K. and Thagard, P. (1989). Analogical Mapping by Constraint Satisfaction. *Cognitive Science* 13: 295–355.

Martin, J. H. (1990). A Computational Model of Metaphor Interpretation. New York: Academic Press.

Mason, Z. J. (2004). CorMet: A Computational, Corpus-Based Conventional Metaphor Extraction System, *Computational Linguistics*, 30(1):23–44.

Shutova, E. (2010a). Models of metaphor in NLP. In *the Proceedings of the 48th Annual Meeting of the Association for Computational Linguistics, Uppsala, Sweden, 688–697.*

Shutova, E. (2010b). Metaphor Identification Using Verb and Noun Clustering. In *the Proc. of the 23rd COLING, the International Conference on Computational Linguistics.*

Veale, T. and Keane, M.T. (1997). The Competence of Sub-Optimal Structure Mapping on 'Hard' Analogies. In *Proceedings of IJCAI'97, the 15th International Joint Conference on Artificial Intelligence,* Nagoya, Japan.

Veale, T. and Hao, Y. (2007). Comprehending and Generating Apt Metaphors: A Web-driven, Case-based Approach to Figurative Language. In *Proc. of the 22nd AAAI conference of the Association for the Advancement of Artificial Intelligence.*

Veale, T. (2012). *Exploding the Creativity Myth: The Computational Foundations of Linguistic Creativity.* London, UK: Bloomsbury/Continuum.

Veale, T. (2014). The ABCs of XYZs: Creativity and Conservativity in Humorous Epithets. *In: J. Manjaly & B. Indurkhya (Eds.) Cognition, Experience, and Creativity.* New Delhi: Orient Blackswan.

Veale, T. (2015). Unnatural Selection: Seeing Human Intelligence in Artificial Creations. *Journal of General Artificial Intelligence* (special issue on Computational Creativity, Concept Invention, and General Intelligence), 6(1):5-20.

Veale, T., Valitutti, A. and Li, G. (2015). Twitter: The Best of Bot Worlds for Automated Wit. In *Proceedings of HCII-2015, the 17th International Conference on Human-Computer Interaction (Distributed, Ambient and Pervasive Interactions),* Los Angeles, California, 2-7.

Way, E. C. (1991). *Knowledge Representation and Metaphor. Studies in Cognitive systems*. Kluwer Academic, Amsterdam.

Wilks, Y. (1978). Making preferences more active. *Artificial Intelligence*, 11(13): 197–223.

Winston, P. (1980)|. Learning and reasoning by analogy. *Communications of the ACM*, 23(12): 689-703.